# MARCELLUS HARTLEY

## A BRIEF MEMOIR

PRINTED PRIVATELY

NEW YORK

1903

# PREFACE

SEVERAL friends of the late Marcellus Hartley, who for the past five and twenty years have been in close business and personal relations with him, believing that a life so useful and patriotic as his should not be allowed to lapse into obscurity, have desired that some memorial of him should be published.

The difficulty of giving interest and color to such a sketch is evident. The life of Mr. Hartley was mainly passed in mercantile pursuits; aside from his files of business letters, he kept no journal and preserved no account of one of the most interesting periods of his career—that which he spent in procuring arms and equipment for the troops called into service during the opening months of the Civil War. Then, too, few men were more reticent; rarely could he be induced to talk on this matter, or, indeed, on any other of a business nature. He seemed to think that the silence imposed upon him when acting in the service of the government was still to be observed long after the occasion had passed. It was only after the day's work, at his country home with a friend on an autumn evening before a blazing fire, or when away on a vacation with mind in repose, that he would tell of his recollections and in his quiet, easy manner charm his listener for hours with anecdotes and incidents of his eventful life.   Enough however, has, it is believed, been gathered together not only to indicate the road along which his success was achieved, but also to give a partial picture of a man of many deeds of charity, most of which will never be known to others than the recipients of his benevolence.   Keeping in mind the quiet demeanor of Mr. Hartley, and feeling that anything concerning him beyond a simple narrative of such incidents of his life as might best serve as a stimulus to others and as a source of interest to his personal friends, would be distasteful to him, the writer of this sketch of his life and work has endeavored to tell the story as simply as possible, in the hope that thereby the narrative may be found not only more characteristic of the man, but all the more fitting a tribute to his memory.

The portraits in this volume represent Mr. Hartley at different periods.   The frontispiece is from a photograph taken about 1896, usually regarded as his best picture.   That opposite page 10, from an old daguerreotype, represents Mr. Hartley as he appeared when a clerk at the age of twenty-one.   That at page 56 shows him at about forty-five years.   Facing pages 58 and 64, are pictures of his home on Orange Mountain and of himself on horseback. The last photograph ever taken of him is reproduced opposite page 70.

Acknowledgments are due to the several friends of Mr. Hartley who have recalled to the mind of the writer many of the incidents he has recorded, to those who have kindly contributed letters and personal tributes, and to Professor William T. Brewster of Columbia University for the reading of proofs.    J. W. H.

GRAMERCY PARK,
   April, 1903.

# CONTENTS

## *Birth, Parentage, and Ancestry*

MARCELLUS HARTLEY was the eldest son of Robert Milham Hartley and Catharine Munson of New York. He was born on the twenty-third of September, 1827, and received the baptismal name of Marcellus from a clergyman of the Dutch Church, an old friend and classmate of his father at Fairfield Academy, where the elder Mr. Hartley had received a classical education with a view to entering the ministry.

Both Mr. Hartley and his wife were descended from ancestors of English origin and of distinguished service. Before the beginning of the sixteenth century the Hartleys were a well-known family in Yorkshire and in several of the northern counties of England. The progenitor of the family from which Robert M. Hartley sprang was the Rev. David Hartley, born in 1674, a graduate of Lincoln College, Oxford, Vicar of Armley, in York, and a highly respected clergyman. Among his children was Dr. David•Hartley (1705–1757), an eminent practitioner, but more famous as a philosopher and metaphysician. He was author of " Observations on Man," and it is from him that Coleridge obtained much philosophical guidance, and for whom he named his eldest son,

Hartley Coleridge. Of his wisdom the poet speaks in
"Religious Musings":

> He of mortal kind
> Wisest, he first who marked the ideal tribes
> Up the fine fibres through the sentient brain.

His son David, a statesman and member of Parliament
for Kingston-on-Hull, was author of many works for the
betterment of the human race. He was the first to in-
troduce into Parliament a bill for the abolition of the
slave-trade, and with Wilberforce followed up the attack
until slavery was banished from the British Empire.
He was, perhaps, more prominently known as a friend
of the American colonies in their struggle for independence, and on the conclusion of the war was appointed by
Lord North to sign the definitive treaty of peace by
which the colonies became free and independent. Of
him Mr. John T. Morse says, in his "Life of Benjamin
Franklin," that he was "a man to whose memory Americans ought to erect statues."

Another son of the Rev. David Hartley, father of the
philosopher, was James Hartley, from whom descended
the subject of the present sketch. Robert, the son of
James Hartley, was born in 1736, and removed from
his home in Lancashire County to Cockermouth in
Cumberland, noted as the birthplace of Wordsworth.
Here he married Martha, daughter of Isaac Smithson,
a member of the family from which also sprang James

Smithson, founder of the Smithsonian Institution at Washington. Among other issue of Robert Hartley was Isaac Hartley, a well-known manufacturer of Cockermouth. It is interesting to note that in early life Isaac Hartley was a schoolmate and companion of the poet Wordsworth, and, though not a poet by training, was a man of imaginative mind, deep sympathy, and devoutness and simplicity of life. In 1787 he married Isabella Johnson. Ten years later, wishing to extend his business, he emigrated to America, and in 1799 sent for his wife and four children. The family settled in Schenectady, New York, and in 1806 Isaac Hartley bought a farm a few miles beyond, at Perth, Fulton County, New York, where he lived till his death, October 6, 1851.

Among his children was Robert Milham Hartley, born in 1796. After spending his boyhood and youth in the country, he removed, about 1822, to New York City, where, after a few years of commercial life, he began a career of philanthropy extending over fifty years. Of uncommonly religious nature, Robert M. Hartley's sympathy was at an early age aroused by the many forms of vice and suffering which he saw in the city; and in the New York Temperance Society, the New York Association for Improving the Condition of the Poor, of which he was a founder and for thirty-three years corresponding secretary, and in several other prominent charities still in active and successful operation, left a worthy name in the records of the history of philanthropy in New York.   Perhaps his most important work was his "Essay on Milk," published in 1842, a vigorous and effective protest against the evil conditions under which that important article of food was produced and distributed.   On many other topics of importance Mr. Hartley also published interesting and valuable tracts; among them were inquiries into the labor question, the industrial education of women, the immigration question, and that of the education of children in the public schools.   All his pamphlets were written from a common-sense and patriotic point of view; they are filled with plain, practical suggestions for the lessening of misery, and they glow with rational zeal for America as a land to live in.   Taken as a whole, they exhibit a growing breadth and interest in the means by which the condition of humanity could, in plain and substantial ways, be improved, and they are the record of an active mind and broadening heart.   It has been necessary to dwell for a moment on this aspect of Mr. Hartley's charities, for the same qualities of growth and expansion and perseverance are, though in a different direction, the most striking facts in the work of his son, Marcellus.

In 1824 Robert M. Hartley married Miss Catharine Munson, the eldest daughter of the Hon. Reuben Munson of New York.   The latter was an enterprising, broad-minded, public-spirited man.   In 1813 he was elected alderman, which post he held for ten successive years, and later became a member of the Assembly. He was also among the founders of many institutions, such as the Bowery Savings Bank, the Tradesmen's National Bank, and was a supporter of several charity organizations. The family from which Mr. Munson sprang was of ancient origin; it had, according to "Burke's Peerage," a history extending over five centuries. Reuben Munson was a direct descendant of Thomas Munson, who came from England and settled in Hartford, Connecticut, in 1637.

On both father's and mother's side, then, Marcellus Hartley was descended from ancient, pure, sturdy stock; his ancestors were all men of integrity and ability, and many of them were uncommonly distinguished for intellectual and moral gifts. If, therefore, Darwin's aphorism be true that "that genius which implies a wonderful, complete combination of high faculties tends to be inherited," it is evident that Mr. Hartley was destined to occupy an important place in life.

# II

*Childhood and Education*
*(1827–1844)*

DETAILS of Marcellus Hartley's youth, such as usually give color and interest to the narrative of a life and show the early traits and molding influences of a character, are rather few. His boyhood was spent in New York. As a child he was not robust, and suffered greatly from headaches, but as he became older his health improved and he grew up after the manner of boys of his day. He enjoyed athletic sports, and excelled particularly in swimming and ball. In this connection, two or three incidents of his youth are interesting. One morning he went with his uncle to the wharf where some produce was unloading which the latter had shipped from his farm. It happened that the docks were wet and slippery, and Marcellus, in crossing from one boat to another, lost his footing and fell into the river. A minute or two elapsed before he was missed; then he appeared swimming quietly after his cap, which was floating away from him. He was promptly hauled out, thoroughly wet, but none the worse for his mishap. On another occasion, while at school in Twenty-seventh Street, he went in swimming,

6

as was the custom of the boys during recess, and had the good fortune, at the peril of his own life, to save a classmate that had ventured too far out in the river, had become exhausted, and was sinking for the last time. Marcellus swam bravely to his rescue, and seizing him by the hair, dragged him safely to shore.

Marcellus Hartley received all his systematic education in the schools of New York City. His longest attendance was at a classical academy occupying the principal floor of Military Hall, 193 Bowery, between Rivington and Delancey streets. Fifty years ago that part of the city was very reputable and was the home of many of our most respected and substantial citizens. The school was under the charge of Rev. Mr. Norton, a cultivated and eminently religious gentleman. Among those who attended the school were Howard Crosby, William E. Dodge, Isaac and Richard Ferris (sons of the old Chancellor of New York University), Peter Naylor, the Porters, Reuben Van Pelt, and two brothers of Marcellus Hartley. Mr. Norton taught them not only the rudimentary branches, but also Latin and Greek preparatory to a college course. He seems to have been an indulgent master.

After the retirement of Mr. Norton from his school, Marcellus Hartley attended a private grammar-school in the basement of the Methodist Church in Seventh Street, under the charge of Clough and Newman. On the discontinuance of that school, he went to Public

School No. 15, in Twenty-seventh Street, near Second Avenue, then practically in the country; for neither Second Avenue nor the side streets above Twenty-eighth Street were opened, and beyond were green fields and rail fences.  This institution stood first among the schools of the old Public School Society, and was under the direction of Anson G. Phelps, Peter Cooper, and James Stokes, one or the other of whom visited it almost daily.  The association of these well-known philanthropists, its high reputation, and the respectable character of its scholars induced Mr. Hartley to place his sons there.  The principal of the school was William A. Walker, a thorough and painstaking educator and a rigorous disciplinarian.  His somewhat nervous temperament found vent in the frequent birching of his pupils.  Marcellus Hartley won his regard and was among the few who escaped castigation.

At these various schools Marcellus Hartley was known among teachers and fellow-students alike as an apt scholar.  He always stood well in his class and was liked by his superiors.  His memory was so good that he rarely forgot anything that he had read, a faculty which stood him in great service in his long business career.  In mathematics and handwriting he excelled; and to his diligence in these studies may be traced the terseness and neatness which in later years distinguished his letters.  Few business men wrote a more beautiful hand, an accomplishment which, uncommon as it is, he retained to the end of his days. Few things, indeed, annoyed him more than to receive a wordy or a badly written letter. Unfortunately, as is too frequently the case with men afterwards eminent, not many of the letters of his youth are preserved.

Marcellus did not pursue his studies systematically after he left Mr. Walker's school. This was in the year 1844; then, at the age of seventeen, he entered his father's office as a clerk.

# III

## *Entry into Business*
## *(1844–1854)*

MARCELLUS HARTLEY remained in his father's employ for three years, and there he obtained a rudimentary knowledge of business. He was ambitious, however, for a more rapid advancement than the outlook promised. Accordingly he sought and soon obtained a situation as entry clerk and assistant bookkeeper in the importing house of Francis Tomes and Sons, of Maiden Lane, dealers in fancy hardware and sporting goods. He entered upon his duties on February 8, 1847. His industry, quickness, and aptness for business enabled him to forge ahead, and he was transferred to the gun department, more congenial to his taste, a branch of business which in later years became the principal factor in his career. In addition, moreover, to duties in the office, he was sent during times when business was slack to solicit trade in the South and the West. These trips were of great service to him in broadening his views. He made the acquaintance of the firm's customers at their homes, and gained a wide knowledge both of the geography and of the business needs of the country. Traveling was in those days much more difficult than it is now, and many hardships fell to the

lot of the itinerant tradesman.  In one of his expedi-
tions, for example, he had a narrow escape from death
by drowning in Lake Erie.  In a letter to a fellow-
clerk, dated December 19, 1851, he gives the following
description of his trials on land and water:

I arrived in Buffalo Wednesday evening and left on Monday evening, and such a time as I had you have no idea of.  I
should not have stayed so long could I have got a good boat;
but, my dear fellow, with all my precaution, and though taking
the best boat on the lake, I came nearer going to the bottom
than ever before.  Enclosed you will find an account of the
total loss of the steamer *Mayflower*, with the list of passengers,
who, thanks to a kind Providence, were all saved.

Such a storm as we had beggars description. . . . Suffice
it to say, I had given up all hope and was waiting patiently for
the boat to founder.  To give you an idea of the weather, the
thermometer was fifteen degrees below zero, the wind blew a
perfect hurricane, the sea went completely over the boat, the
spray freezing as it rose in the air and so completely envelop-
ing us that it was impossible to see twenty feet from the
steamer.  Food I never tasted for twenty-six hours, until we
struck the shore, which occurred at eleven o'clock at night. . . .
When we struck nobody knew where we were, nor did we
much care, for then we never expected to reach land.  But
when morning came and we saw the shore some two hundred
feet from us,—a high bleak coast with a ridge of ice eight feet
high all along the shore, the sea running mountains high,—we
had hopes of reaching it, and with the assistance of some persons from the shore we eventually sent a line, and once more
safely reached *terra firma*.  My baggage was wet and freezing,
but that was of little account.  We had to walk a mile through
snow a foot deep and then ride twelve miles to the nearest
staging, where I took passage for the first railroad station,

Painesville. When I tell you that I came near breaking my neck twice you will think I am unlucky. We were upset twice in the stage and went over a bank some six feet high, the last time being about four o'clock in the morning. Cold ! It was awfully cold. . . . We footed it through the snow some half mile to a farmer's house, who kindly gave us shelter and fire until morning. Sleep ! I had none since leaving Buffalo, three evenings before, until last night (Thursday), and but two meals in three days. Such, my dear friend, has been my fortune so far; and through it all I have come out, thanks to a kind Providence, with but a frozen foot, one finger frost-bitten, and with my phrenological bump of veneration raised considerable by the upsetting of the stage.

Here I am in Cleveland with a comfortable, fine bedroom and a parlor, with my feet bound up, which will probably keep me in the hotel for three or four days, with nothing to do but to read and write letters. . . .

The journey before me is a tedious and uncomfortable one, far different from my summer experience. From here it is my intention to go to Detroit, Chicago, St. Louis, and down to Memphis. I am going as far as Montgomery or New Orleans; probably I may visit both. It is now nearly twelve o'clock, and I am tired. The writing you will please excuse, as my fingers are somewhat frost-bitten.

The following extract from a letter is worthy of insertion, since it gives an idea of the sort of impression made upon Mr. Hartley's wide-awake intelligence by the Western cities and towns which he visited in his business trips:

CHICAGO, June 15, 1851.

*My dear Brother:*

I arrived in this place this morning, from Detroit. The last I wrote you was a few hurried lines from Buffalo. My journey so far has been very agreeable: the trip through Lake Erie was beautiful. From Buffalo I went direct to Cleveland, where I remained for two days, heard the Reverend John Marsh of New York preach, and Gough make a speech. There is no city in this country that will compare to Cleveland. It would be the place precisely for Uncle Booth. I, however, became somewhat tired of it, having nobody to walk about with me. From Cleveland I went to Sandusky, and then to Toledo. The sail from place to place was beautiful, but the two last-mentioned places were very dull. At the entrance of the Maumee River there is a place called Manhattan, having a church, mill, and some thirty fine houses, three or four large warehouses, canal and wharves, etc.,—in fact, the miniature of a young city,—but the population of that place numbers but one family. During the speculations of 1837, the land was in the hands of New York speculators, who laid it out into town lots, and sold them for $1000 to $5000 a lot, built houses, established a bank, extended the canal, intending it should be the city of the West; but now all that remains of its former activity are its vacant houses and its grass-growing streets, a warning to all land speculators. Toledo, a few miles beyond it, is a thriving place and will eventually become a city of celebrity. All through that portion of Ohio known as the "Reserve lands" there have been towns and cities laid out, and if you will look upon the map you will see Independence, Napoleon, etc., printed in large letters, as if they were places with some thousands of inhabitants, but you might ride through them a dozen times and fail to discover them, for they contain but some half dozen or more houses. On the route from Toledo to Detroit there is another place of that description called Munroe in Michigan. It is some three miles from the lake, on the Raisin River. They went to the enormous expense of making a ship-canal to the lake, have a railroad, etc., but the place now it would trouble you to find. I arrived at Detroit last Thursday night, and remained there until Saturday morning. I was very much pleased with it; you know it is an old settlement, and the houses, and the appearance of things generally, put one in mind of the Eastern cities. In most of the cities that I have visited West the houses are chiefly frame—that is, wood. Now in Detroit they have commenced the use of brick, so also here in Chicago. You have no idea of the Western country. You might be in Chicago, or any of these Western cities and towns, and think you were in the State of New York. A man with money, or a go-ahead Eastern man, could soon become a millionaire. I find that my time will not allow me to go to Milwaukee and further West, as I intended, but shall go from here through Illinois to St. Louis.

Mr. Hartley's perils were not all of the deep, nor were his experiences confined to his travels. He often related the exciting scene he witnessed at the Astor Place Riots in the spring of 1850, and the danger he was in. When Macready, the English actor, was playing *Macbeth* in New York, a gang of turbulent fellows known as the "Bowery boys" determined to take vengeance upon him for an alleged insult which the American tragedian, Edwin Forrest, had received in England the year before. Repelled in an attempt to invade the opera-house, they turned on the police who opposed them, assaulted them with sticks and stones, and seriously wounded many. Getting the better of the police, they next attacked the Seventh Regiment, which had been hastily summoned, and handled it so roughly that the soldiers, as a last resort, were obliged to use their guns. When the street was cleared some twenty rioters and several spectators were killed, fifty were seriously wounded, and a hundred and fifty officers and men were more or less badly hurt. The beginning of the fray Mr. Hartley saw from a lamp-post, but when the firing began dropped to the ground. How he escaped without a scratch was a source of wonder to his friends.

In addition to his business, Mr. Hartley was alive in other ways. When, in 1850, the Hungarian patriot Kossuth visited this country, Mr. Hartley was much interested in him as a man and an orator, and became a deep sympathizer with the wrongs which his country suffered. He also joined a society, the object of which, as given in its ambitious constitution, "was the discussion of literary subjects and the promotion of literature, science, and friendship among its members." The club had a properly fitted room where the members could go at any time, and where every fortnight they held evening sessions for debate on popular subjects of the day. Most of the members afterwards became well-known and highly respected citizens, but of the little coterie of kindred spirits only eight are living. After a lapse of so many years no apology need be made for mentioning their names; for, should they happen to see this allusion to them, it will recall the old "Philosophian" and awaken a thrill of joy for those happy days of their youth when

> Hope grew round me like the twining vine,
> And fruits and flowers not my own, seemed mine.

Their names are Edward M. Townsend, David S.

Egleston, Abraham R. Lawrence, Henry L. Pierson, Joseph W. Hartley, Hewlet Scudder, Robert Beloni, and George Fuller.

Mr. Hartley, of course, had his days of discouragement. He, however, seems never seriously to have considered any change of occupation, but, in order to work to the best advantage, he left the firm of Francis Tomes and Sons, in 1854, and entered business for himself.

# IV

## *The Beginning of a Career*
## *(1854–1862)*

THOUGH it was a bold undertaking for a young
man without means or influential friends to enter
business for himself, Mr. Hartley was moved to that act
by several reasons. During his service as clerk he
had, in upwards of seven years, mastered all the details
of the department — that of sporting guns — of which he
was in charge. Having obtained all the knowledge of
the business that he could, and believing from the conditions which he saw about him that there was no opportunity of his ever becoming a partner, he perceived the
uselessness of his remaining longer in his position.

Accordingly, his first step was to find men of similar
disposition. These he met in J. Rutsen Schuyler and
Malcolm Graham, who were in the firm of Smith, Young
and Company, of which Mr. Schuyler was junior partner;
they were engaged in the same line of business as Francis Tomes and Sons. One day the three met at the
famous hostelry kept by Clark and Brown in Maiden
Lane, near its junction with Liberty Street. Here the
young men discussed the feasibility of establishing a
new business firm of the same sort as that of their em-

ployers, and, concluding that it was possible, immediately entered into the details. Since the three partners were without much money, they were obliged to borrow a large part of their capital. With this, the firm was organized on March 1, 1854, under the name of Schuyler, Hartley, and Graham, and took the ground floor of 13 Maiden Lane, nearly opposite the parent firms. Mr. Hartley's part in the business, owing to his long experience in buying and selling goods away from home, consisted chiefly in the purchase of a varied stock in trade, especially sporting guns and small arms abroad, and in trips West for the purpose of creating a market for his wares.

Almost as soon as the firm was fully organized, Mr. Schuyler and Mr. Hartley, fortified with a letter of credit on Brown, Shipley, and Company, of London, started for Europe to purchase a supply of goods for the new store, leaving Mr. Graham to look after their interests at home. They took passage on the fourth of March, 1854, in the steamer *Baltic*. They visited all the important dealers and manufacturers in their line of business, both in England and on the Continent, bought the newest goods, and made arrangements for future supplies as they might be required. They remained abroad about four months. The goods which they shipped from Europe and brought with them they had no difficulty in selling at a large profit. The success of the firm was assured.

During the winter following, Mr. Hartley made a business trip West, and thereby considerably enlarged the amount of the firm's undertakings. The following year, in April, Mr. Hartley again went to England and the Continent for fresh goods, and his trip was repeated in 1856 and 1857 with unfailing success. He established close relations with the leading firms in Europe, and acquired knowledge about the manufacture and sale of arms which enabled him to render notable service to the United States Government during the Civil War.

On his return from his last trip in the autumn of 1857, Mr. Hartley found the country convulsed by the severest financial panic it had ever experienced. New York, as the business center of the nation, was the first to feel the effects of the storm, which, however, extended rapidly and with devastating force over the whole country. In a calamity which produced no less than nine hundred and eighty-five business failures in the metropolis alone, with liabilities exceeding one hundred and twenty millions, which caused banks to suspend payment, and brought business to a standstill, Mr. Hartley's firm weathered the storm successfully. Indeed, in the following three years of 1858, 1859, and 1860, during which Mr. Hartley remained in New York, the business of the firm increased in importance and extent from year to year, and became the largest of its kind in the country. Inasmuch as the increase was owing chiefly to the purchase and sale of arms, Mr. Hartley had to give a great deal of his time to that branch of the business, in which he was the specialist.

The operations of the firm were not, however, wholly confined to munitions of war. To show the adroitness with which its members seized opportunities, one or two incidents may be mentioned. On his third trip to Europe, Mr. Hartley, knowing the great demand that existed at that time for coral ornaments, bought up all the coral that he could find in the markets of southern Europe. The monopoly which his firm thus enjoyed during the great vogue of the article yielded large profits. At another time, when in Florence looking for suitable goods for his business, he was attracted by a window filled with copies of the old masters, and inquired the price of the most beautiful. Finding it too high, he was about to leave, but the dealer called him back and named a lower figure. This was still too high, nor did the dealer succeed in lowering his price enough to suit Mr. Hartley, who departed. Disappointed, the dealer followed Mr. Hartley to his hotel, but again Mr. Hartley declined to make any bid. With the pleasant persistence and love of driving a bargain characteristic of Italian shopkeepers, the man followed him to the next city and again sought to reopen the negotiations at a still lower figure. Finally Mr. Hartley asked the dealer how many pictures he had, and having ascertained the number,— it was a moderate-sized shopful,—the names of the various pictures, and the alleged painters, he suddenly asked the dealer how much he would take for the whole lot. The latter was at first amazed at the supposed banter, but, assured of Mr. Hartley's sincerity, named prices about one quarter of those of the first interview. To the astonishment and possibly the consternation of the Italian, Mr. Hartley bought the entire stock. He had the pictures boxed, and, though they would have almost filled a small vessel, got them home safely in a few months. On his return he succeeded in selling his "old masters" to his customers West and South, at a large profit, without, however, representing them to be other than copies.

A few words must be said regarding the more personal life of Mr. Hartley. In the fall of 1855 he was married to Frances Chester White, second daughter of Dr. Samuel Pomeroy White and Caroline Mary Jenkins of New York. They were married by the Rev. Dr. William Adams of the Madison Square Presbyterian Church, where the families of both had long attended. Dr. White, the son of Dr. Samuel White, was in early life a physician at Hudson, New York; thence he removed to this city, where he continued successfully the practising of his profession. Mrs. Hartley's mother was a granddaughter of Seth Jenkins, first mayor of Hudson, who, with his brother, Thomas, was the founder of that city, and daughter of Robert Jenkins, who started the first cotton-mill in the State. The latter was for ten years the mayor of Hudson, and occupied other positions of honor and trust.

Up to the time of his marriage, Mr. Hartley had

always lived with his father, and for a short time after
his marriage he and his wife made their residence at the
elder Mr. Hartley's house. It would, indeed, be impossible to exaggerate the reverence of the son for his
parents and the affection of the parents for the son.
"This day," wrote the father in the journal which he was
accustomed throughout his life to keep— "this day, Marcellus, with his wife, has left his father's house, the only
home he has ever known, for a permanent abode elsewhere. My heart has been touched by this separation.
Oh! the instability of all earthly things! The nearest
and dearest ties exist but to be broken. I have commended him to God, praying and trusting that we may
all yet, in the covenant of His grace, be gathered around
His throne, an unbroken family in heaven."

When, in the spring of the following year, Mr. Hartley
made his third trip to Europe, he took his wife with him.
They visited the principal places of interest in England
and on the Continent, and Mr. Hartley's personal letters
of this period are longer and more varied than at any
subsequent time of his life. Some of them reveal his
character and his way of looking at things in so interesting a manner that it is well to quote a few lines.
They are the impressions of a young American who
went abroad in the early fifties, at a time when traveling was not so easy and when a trip to Europe was
by no means so commonplace a thing as it is to-day.
On July 22, 1855, in a letter to his sister, he gives

some interesting impressions of Cockermouth, the home
of his ancestors, and of the neighboring region:

My first impressions of Cockermouth you no doubt would
like to hear. I must say that they were very unfavorable. It
looked like some old, wornout city. . . . Cockermouth is situated
on the south side of the river Derwent and at the mouth of
the river Cocker. . . . The river, like all English rivers,
is very small. The Derwent is about the size of Uncle
John's creek, some places running deep, and others shallow
enough to cross from stone to stone without wetting your feet.
There are but three churches in the place, one Episcopal, Con-
gregational, and Methodist; the old church was burned down
some years ago, but now they have a very pretty stone one
built in the shape of a cross. I attended service there this
morning.

To a stranger all that is interesting in Cockermouth is the
castle and the house in which the poet Wordsworth was born.
The country round about is beautiful, but the view from your
gate, to my mind, is far more grand. At Cockermouth you
begin to reach that portion of Cumberland which is considered
the classic ground of England. Keswick is only twelve miles
from here. I shall return by that route, passing through the
finest portion of England, and, if I am to believe the poets and
some English travelers, unsurpassed by any other place in the
world,—of course the world so far as they had seen. I will not
admit any such conception until I see it for myself, and then
compare it with what I have seen in my own country. The
poets of England should have visited America before they
used the comprehensive word "world."

I resume this letter from this place [Birmingham, July 26],
but only have a few moments to write. I left Cockermouth
on Monday morning by stage to Keswick, and visited all places
of interest—Windermere, Ambleside, Kendal, and Derwent.
It was a most beautiful ride, a picture in comparison to our

wild and extensive rivers, lakes, and mountains, a lovely land-scape—everything so diminished in size that you have nature in miniature, as it were.

In a letter written to his mother, May 19, 1856, from Trieste we read an interesting account of his impressions of Italy, particularly of Venice:

Milan is a very pretty place, the neatest and cleanest city in Italy save Venice. The country through Tuscany, Sardinia, and Lombardy is a garden, and all it wants to make it a great and enterprising country is education and union among the different countries. Venice is a beautiful city, and novel. Instead of streets they have canals on which, you are aware, they use the famous gondolas. Fanny was charmed, and did not like to leave it. We could only spend Sunday there, as my time is precious and I ought to be in Paris. The weather for the last ten days previous to our arrival at Venice had been disagreeable, raining incessantly, but at Venice we had fine weather and everybody appeared to enjoy it. The canals, or streets, were alive with gondolas. Sunday with the Venetians is a holiday, and from our windows the sight was grand. Our hotel was on the Grand Canal, within sight of the Church of San Marco. The Rialto was in the distance. On the canal were hundreds of gondolas following a barge filled full of Austrian musicians, drawn by two gaily decked gondolas. It was about seven o'clock in the evening. All Venice had collected in their boats to take a ride and hear the music. We were not disturbed by the noise of horses and vehicles. It was as quiet as if you had been to sea in a calm. The sight was grand, yet it turned my thoughts to my own country, where we venerate the Sabbath. I thought that had the Venetians attended more to the observance of the Divine Laws, they, in common with the rest of Italy, would have more to boast of at the present day than the ruins and dilapidations of their city, once the pride of the world.

Mr. and Mrs. Hartley returned to America in the fall of the same year. These yearly visits to Europe marked the beginning of a career of uncommon activity and success, the first and most engaging episode of which will be treated in the next chapter.

# V

## *Work for the Cause of the Union* (*1862–1864*)

THE period of the Civil War is probably the most
interesting time of Mr. Hartley's life, but, unfortunately, the reticence which he maintained with regard
to his work as special agent for the government during
that struggle prevented him from speaking of his experiences. Consequently our information is somewhat
meager; what we know is chiefly from his business letters. We have seen how his firm weathered the financial
crisis of 1857; in 1860 another fierce money panic broke
out, and the business of the country was paralyzed by
the approaching danger of war. Again Mr. Hartley's
firm withstood the shock successfully, and indeed, owing
to the special nature of its business,—the selling of arms
and munitions of war,— was enabled to make money.

A brief explanation should be given of the conditions
of the time. For some years back the South had been
silently preparing for the coming conflict. The slavery
men had got possession of all the arms and munitions
of war that they could; and it is certain that the South
at the beginning of 1861 was in a much better condition than was the North for a contest. Now, it was
natural that in a time of such strong feeling and grow-

ing bitterness, a firm like Mr. Hartley's, in part because undoubtedly making profit by the sale of arms, should suffer much embarrassment in doing business of that sort when the loyalty of almost every man, however patriotic, was more or less under suspicion. It happened that the jealousy of competitors and of sympathizers with the South threw every possible obstacle in the way of the firm. Indeed, some rivals went so far as to cite the firm before the grand jury; they charged it with the selling of goods to the South, and a cordon of police was placed before the store to watch each shipment of arms as it went out. Such an indignity to a respectable firm, every member of which was loyal to the core, Mr. Hartley met firmly and promptly. He went to the grand jury, taking with him the sale and shipping books of the firm for a year. These were carefully examined; it was found not only that no sales had been made to the South, but that sales which bore suspicion of being intended for clandestine shipment had been cancelled and the goods given to western states about whose loyalty there could be no question. The charge was therefore dismissed and the firm commended for its uprightness. Subsequently it was ascertained that this act was inspired by the enemies of the government, who, in this manner, hoped to retard and embarrass the loyal states in obtaining arms for their troops.

By the middle of 1861 it became apparent that the

war was to assume far larger proportions than had been dreamed of. The work of equipping an army of a million men, which Congress authorized in response to President Lincoln's message of July, was entirely beyond the experience of any men of modern times; for, large as were the armies of Europe during the Napoleonic wars and former fierce conflicts, no single power ever called for so many troops to be marshaled in so short a time. One of the gravest problems which confronted the Secretary of War, Mr. Stanton, was the arming of this vast force of men.

The difficulty lay in the fact that the arsenals had been denuded of their guns. The stock in the hands of the dealers was insufficient, and manufacturers, although driven to their utmost capacity, were unable to furnish a tithe of what were required. In this difficulty, Mr. Stanton called to his aid his friend, Robert Dale Owen, a man widely known as of practical sagacity, undoubted loyalty, and irreproachable integrity. Him Mr. Stanton commissioned to go to New York and there to confer with Governor Morgan as to the most reliable and competent person to be appointed as agent of the United States Government to purchase arms and munitions of war in Europe.

The choice fell upon Mr. Hartley. With the approval of the Secretary of War, then personally unknown to him, and with the consent of President Lincoln, he was made agent with a rank equivalent to that of brigadier-general, and was given a large credit on Baring Brothers, the fiscal agents of the government. To Mr. Hartley the appointment came as a surprise, and, since his acceptance would greatly harm his business interests, he might well have hesitated. As a member of a firm whose traffic was mainly directed to the buying and selling of arms, his time, experience, and ability were invaluable to it. If, however, there was one virtue in the character of Mr. Hartley more pronounced than another, it was his patriotism. His patriotism, indeed, was inborn. No sacrifice was too great for him to make when he could serve his country. He would permit no selfish consideration to come between him and the exercise of his loyalty. All was to be subordinated to the higher and nobler duty of service to his native land in the hour of her supreme peril. Accordingly, he accepted the flattering but onerous position.

Having settled business with his partners and arranged his private affairs, he set out for Europe in July, 1862, accompanied by his family, for what proved to be a stay of some months. He went directly to Birmingham, and took a house which he made the headquarters for his operations. Little, however, did he realize the difficulties which would beset him in carrying out the object of his mission. His instructions were remarkably simple: he was not only to buy all available guns and munitions of war, but to prevent any falling into the hands of the Confederate Government. The carrying out of the order was not so easy. His first great obstacle lay in the temper of the English people. He had thought that in England, at least, he should find the majority of men in sympathy with the North in a war waged for the integrity of the Union, whereas the South's avowed object was its destruction and the organization of a government with slavery as its chief corner-stone. On the contrary, he found in England a wide-spread spirit of hostility; hence the difficulties in his way were very great. Another obstacle was the fact that arms were to be bought in all countries of Europe, and that Confederate agents were abroad in the land buying what they could for Confederate armies. He soon found, therefore, that his chief task was not merely the purchasing of arms for the United States Government, but also the circumventing of Confederate agents and the overcoming, incidentally, of hostile public opinion in England. In all these respects Mr. Hartley was successful. A few letters and illustrations may be given to show the character of his work.[1] Immediately after his arrival in England he wrote to the Secretary of War as follows:

> 6 ST. MARY'S ROW,
> BIRMINGHAM, August 2, 1862.

Dear Sir:

I arrived in Birmingham Saturday, July 26, and found that our agent had secured all the ready-made rifles at prices quoted by me, and the services of nearly all the manufac-

---

[1] Other characteristic letters are printed in the Appendix, pages 130-149.

turers. Nearly all the ready-made guns had been bought up by speculators immediately on receipt of the news of the want of 300,000 more men. The London market had been cleaned out by speculators for the China trade. In this market Henderson, an American, had made contracts with nearly all the manufacturers at low prices, and is now holding them to it, some 36/ to 40/, a loss in many instances to the manufacturers; our agent succeeded in obtaining some from them at an advanced price, but as they hope to complete contracts this week and we have secured them, and the arms go to New York, it is better that we should *get him* out the way.

The Small Arms Company, a combination of manufacturers who produce about 3000 per week, have given the refusal of their " Combination " to a New York house with hopes of obtaining a Government contract at $17. They expect to receive an answer by the mail now due, on receipt of which I hope to close a contract with them before my departure for the Continent. I offered them 47/6, but as they were not in condition to close I withdrew my offer.

In a week or so, when we get things under way and can obtain the control of the " Combination," I hope to send 4000 to 5000 per week, and will swell the amount to 6000 and upwards when under full headway.

Our agent had secured, before my arrival, some 2000 ready at 45/ to 46/6. There were some 2000 more in the hands of speculators, for which they asked 60/ to 63/, which for the present we shall let them hold.

Previous to the news of the want of additional troops, rifles were a drug, and manufacturers took contracts at a low price in order to work up the surplus material. The speculators took advantage of it and bound them down. Now when they have to give orders for materials prices advance, and the greater the pressure the higher the price, so we have to manage quietly, in order to get them under full headway without pressing the material makers too sharply.

Where arms are contracted for and going to New York, I

have not interfered, as the sooner we get them out of the way
the better, as I have secured the services of the manufacturers.
It will not do to pay over $15 in New York; if it is done, it
will have the effect of speculators obtaining arms from our
manufacturers. I shall not for the present give over 50/ for
arms, as the speculators are so combined together that they
turn over their guns into one another's hands and thus manage to obtain the highest price.

Most of the arms made and on hand are 57.7 calibre, and are
not of as good quality as I shall have when we get under way
and shall make such changes as I can make them agree to, corresponding to our Springfield.

So far everything has worked most successfully for nearly
the whole produce of this market, and it will take a little time
to get it systematized and under way. I should much prefer to
obtain the whole amount in this market of one kind of arms,
with such as are ready made on the Continent, than to contract
all over the Continent on time.

I was at the London Armory Company on Wednesday, and
they promised to give me an answer this morning how many
they could furnish and the price, but they have failed to do so.
I shall see them on Monday, as I pass through London on my
way to Liège.

My credit of £80,000 will soon be exhausted; it will not purchase over 30,000 to 35,000 arms, and if I succeed in purchasing some in Liège, where I have the refusal of a lot, I shall not
have more than enough to cover one month's purchases. Please
lose no time in sending me an additional credit of at least
£100,000, say one hundred thousand pounds, same terms as
before. Send by return steamer; my house in New York will
send it.

The vessels from Liverpool are crowded with freight, so that
goods have to be there some days before the arrival of a
steamer, in order to secure their turn. I shall make a shipment next week.

Agreeably to instructions, I have detailed to you my first week's work, and shall continue to inform you of my progress, and hope that nothing will interfere to prevent me from realizing my anticipations, say some 6000 per week.

Yours respectfully,

MARCELLUS HARTLEY.

To Hon. E. M. STANTON,
    Secretary of War.

The energy with which he threw himself into his business appears in the following two letters. The first expresses the magnitude of the undertaking; the second deals with his knowledge of the market and the means which he saw were necessary to prevent the government from becoming the prey of monopolies and speculators. Both are very practical and sagacious.

6 St. MARY'S ROW,<br>BIRMINGHAM, August 6, 1862.

HON. P. H. WATSON.
    *My dear Sir:*

By this mail I write a detailed account, and send the same to the Secretary of War. The Henderson who secured in the market at the low prices is the same man who operated for H. and A. last year. Everything thus far has worked splendidly, and I am only waiting for the Small Arms Company to learn by next mail that the contract they expect is among the things that might have occurred, to secure the entire product of this market. I have remained in the background, allowing our agent, Mr. Tomes, to secure the manufacturers. I have seen several who expect a friend from New York with large government contracts: Tomes, Barkalow, etc., are mentioned. You will please see that I have more credit at once. I do not want to contract beyond the £80,000, as I shall then be held personally responsible, which of course is no risk, yet under the circumstances the government should cover me promptly. I am at work in earnest; it is a laborious job. I shall leave our agent to take care of things until I obtain what are ready made on the Continent. I have the refusal of some 2000 in Liège.

I enclose two slips cut from the Birmingham "Daily Post" and the London "Times," about shipping munitions of war to Southern States. The steamer *Memphis* is now loading at Liverpool with munitions of war for Nassau, or some adjacent port convenient to some Southern port; as nearly as I can find out, she has about 3000 rifles on board.

I shall do my utmost to send all arms at once, without delay. I think I shall be able to obtain all in this market at prices varying from 45/ to 50/, unless orders from some Continental power make them advance, and in that case we may have to allow a little even with those with whom we have contracts made, for the manufacturers are a slippery set.

Respectfully yours,

MARCELLUS HARTLEY.

---

47 HAMPTON STREET,
BIRMINGHAM, November 29, 1862.

CAPT. S. CRISPIN.

*My dear Sir:*

. . . The effect of advancing guns on your side was the advancing here. I was a little mortified to find it had been done. You did not obtain one more gun for it. It enabled the purchasers to go right over me, and I did not understand it until I had written to New York about it. The policy should have been to act in unison with me. You should have notified me that on such a day you intended to put the price at $14.50

or stop buying. The importers would have at once telegraphed or written. Send no more guns except at a very low price, or send no more at all. I should have been indifferent about buying for a few days, but would finally conclude to buy on speculation, provided they would sell at, say, 42/; and I would agree to take all they had made and under way at that price, with the positive understanding, binding in writing, that they would agree to furnish me all they could make for one, two, or three months, as the case might be, at the same price. They would have jumped at it. Do you know that prior to my arrival the Small Arms Company offered 15,000 Enfields at 45/, and had it not been for the contract made with them through Naylor at Washington I could have purchased them at that price? Parties complained at Washington that I was advancing the price of Enfields. The fact was that they at Washington were doing that very thing, and those who had any to sell, of course, said it was I. When I say "you," in referring to the purchase above, I refer to the "powers that are." They should have left you and me to manage this thing.

When Mr. Inman shut down on carrying munitions of war by his vessels, all the shippers and buyers stopped, and not being in a position myself to go on very freely, I slackened up; the consequence was that in one week guns went to 42/, and even lower here. I purchased some yesterday at 42/. Henderson purchased some as low as 38/, but they are very inferior. That shows who keeps the price up. The Small Arms Company have been in the market buying at 42/ to 48/ to send to New York. They will make a good thing out of it. This company have managed their affairs very nicely. They have informed the department in Washington that all arms not made by them, or that do not come through them, are the "rejects." They have advanced the price of materials and stocking, occasioned by the increased price given to Naylor, and, of course, how can I buy for less than 50/ if they have managed things so as to cut off the outside manufacturers from buying by advancing the price? They are up to all manner of tricks, and I hope you will exert your influence in order that Naylor may not get another contract. When I came here I went to London to see what I could do with the wealthy manufacturers, and Swinburne, the manager of the Small Arms Company, telegraphed to London, asking the refusal of all their arms at 60/ for one week. He telegraphed to four parties. They, understanding his tricks, showed me the telegrams, knowing at once what his object has been and is.

At the breaking out of our difficulties, when our Mr. Schuyler first went into the market, we had made purchases from our regular manufacturers at 45/. When the demand was urgent, and Crowninshield and Howland and Aspinwall and our Mr. Schuyler were here, the Small Arms Company put the price at 100/, and kept it at 80/ for months. They bought up all in the market, and did their utmost to drive all the manufacturers into their combination. Mr. Schuyler then started about thirty-five manufacturers outside of their combination. He put their price down, and from that time to this we have obtained more guns out of their combination than they have made in it, two-fold. I hope you will break it up and give them what they deserve. We have done our best to break it up, and had we not started the outsiders you would have been paying at least 75/ to-day for every gun.

I received a letter to-day from Mr. Schuyler telling me to send the material to the firm. It is better, I think, to do so, as I have really no authority to purchase them. Yet still, they could have no objection. When you make a change try and inform me in time, if possible, that I may take advantage of it. I have written this very rapidly. I do not often write such long scrawls, but I hope you will be able to decipher it.

> With best wishes from
> Yours truly and sincerely,
>
> M. HARTLEY.

The mention of Mr. Inman in the foregoing letter brings up another interesting episode in Mr. Hartley's business arrangements. Toward the end of October the amount of arms of which he had gained control or had bought outright became so large that he thought of chartering a special steamer to ship them to America. Accordingly, he asked his bankers to make inquiries, in a covert manner, of Mr. Inman and other steamship owners to see if the affair could be carried through. Meanwhile he wrote to all his agents on the Continent, bidding them hold in readiness for instant shipment all the arms they had on hand or could collect. The amount of his planning and correspondence over the affair was very large and the details intricate. For some reason, possibly that hinted at in the foregoing letters, the project was never realized, and Mr. Hartley continued to send guns to America by the usual method.

The following extract from a letter to Mr. Stanton, dated from Birmingham, August 30, 1862, illustrates another sort of difficulty with which he had to contend, and is an example of the soundness of his views:

The Small Arms Company referred to in my letters several times I am led to believe have been deceiving us. They are sending arms South, not direct, but they have made a contract with some party. They have been doing it somewhat previous to my arrival. They have also been sending some to parties North under contract; but the bulk of what they make, say 2000 at least per week, are going to Liverpool to be sent to Nassau.  I would respectfully suggest the increasing of our force in that vicinity.  The secretary of the company assured me last week that he would be able to sell me arms in a week, and in a month the product of his factory, and, in answer to my inquiry "that I hoped he was sending his arms North," replied, "Yes, all," but I have learned since that he told what was not so.  I shall not, from present appearances, obtain over 70,000 Enfield rifles by the 1st of November.  If it is your desire to extend the time and increase the number over 100,000, please let me know as soon as possible.  If we relinquish our manufacturers, it will be difficult to obtain them again; or if they do not take other contracts, when my engagements with them cease, it will take some time to get them under way, if we relinquish and then go on.  Some are now enquiring that they may get their stock ready.  I have always advocated the policy of the United States Government taking the whole English Enfield market from the beginning of this war.  First, they are the best guns.  Secondly, we should have kept them from the South.  It is not too late now.  It would be money well invested.  There is no other market for the South for good arms.  All the Continental manufacturers are full of government orders, and as this is the only market they—the South—have, I respectfully suggest that it would be the policy of our government to so secure the good arms that we may have them, and that we should keep them from the South, at least for some little time.  It would not take much money, but it would be well expended.  You will pardon me for referring to this matter, but I have thought it of sufficient importance to call your attention to it.

From England Mr. Hartley went to the Continent, where, during September and October, he spent three or four weeks in visiting the chief manufacturing cities in order to lay hold of the supply of arms.  As we know from the last extract, he virtually controlled the output on the Continent, and his letters to Secretary Stanton are replete with the details of his purchases in Berlin, Cologne, Paris, and other cities. The following is an interesting episode of his work.

While Mr. Hartley was in Birmingham, he learned that the agents of the Confederate Government had made a contract with some gun manufacturers on the Continent for several thousand rifles. He was determined to prevent the delivery of these arms. With little to guide him but a general knowledge of the various Continental manufacturers, he immediately started out to discover the sellers. At Vienna, Frankfort, and Budapest he was disappointed; but finally, at Liège, he found, to his joy, the object of his search. Without making his position known, he interviewed the firm, and in the course of a general conversation learned the facts of the case and all the necessary particulars. Then, disclosing his position as the agent of the United States, he offered to buy the rifles at a small advance over the price for which they had been sold to the agents of the South, and to pay for them on bill-of-lading by drafts on his London bankers.

The unscrupulous manufacturers accepted his offer and the arms were turned over to the North. But Mr. Hartley's work was not done. A firm which, for a little more gain, would prove false to a contract made in good faith, was not to be trusted. So Mr. Hartley remained in

Liège long enough to see the arms safely shipped. When, however, the time came for the payment for the goods, Mr. Hartley found himself in some embarrassment. In his anxiety to prevent the guns from falling into the hands of the Confederates, he had agreed to pay cash for them by drafts on his bankers, though knowing that they were not in funds. Hastening to London, he at once saw his bankers and explained to them what he had done, and sent word to the Secretary of War, who immediately authorized the payment of the drafts. Mr. Hartley then returned to Liège, and settled matters with the manufacturers.

The effect of such work as this is illustrated by the following story. At a dinner given by Mr. Charles R. Flint, a close friend of Mr. Hartley's, to a London banker, Mr. John Dennistown, Mr. Hartley and a Mr. Trenholm were present. This Mr. Trenholm had been, during the Civil War, a resident agent in Europe of the Confederate Government, and at the close of the war had come North. At the dinner he made a speech. After alluding to the kindness and courtesy he had received from the people of the North during his residence among them, and paying tribute to their shrewdness and enterprise, he gave a graphic description of the difficulty he had experienced in obtaining arms in Europe for the Confederate Government. Among other things, he said that at times he was on the point of securing all that he required, but through some unknown agency, which he had never been able to discover, his efforts had been constantly frustrated. He then told the very incident which has just been related. Mr. Flint, who had heard Mr. Hartley relate the story, drew from Mr. Trenholm, in the course of his remarks that followed, more of the details of the affair, and having obtained all the facts, remarked that the gentleman to whom Mr. Trenholm alluded was one of his guests at the table. Mr. Hartley, as much astonished as Mr. Trenholm at the outcome of the matter, arose, acknowledged the fact, and for the first time explained to Mr. Trenholm and the guests exactly what he had done. Thus Mr. Hartley, amid much enthusiasm and to his surprise, became the hero of the hour.

Although Mr. Hartley's time and thought were chiefly employed in buying arms and munitions of war for the equipment of the army, he lost no opportunity, as has been said, for strengthening the moral side of the cause of the North, and endeavoring to make the British people more sympathetic to that cause. It will be well, at this point, to quote from a letter which he wrote to his brother in the fall of 1862, from London, since this letter explains something of the difficulty he had encountered not only in sending goods to market, but also in the attitude of the English:

I am in receipt of your two letters and would have written to you before but I have had but little time to devote to private correspondence. I have been here located with my family for two weeks, occasionally running up to Birmingham. I am bothered with the shipping of my goods, and, to crown it all, Mr. Inman refuses to allow his vessels to load goods contraband of war. But business I must not speak about.

As a calm and distant observer of affairs in our country, I must say that the energy that has heretofore been characteristic of us as a nation now appears to me to lie dormant. Of course, none of us know what the leaders have to contend with, but it seems to me that we do not make headway. I am mortified to find that men who call themselves "loyal Americans" . . . are trying to throw obstacles in the way of the government, as if the government had not enough to contend with already; that the great Democratic party, to whose auspices and administration we are indebted for the breaking out of this cursed rebellion, . . . the great Democratic party, made up of those who will not fight, and the disloyal people seeking shelter under the flag of the Union, is taking the opportunity to embarrass the government, is raising false issues and perverting the truth, and is now endeavoring to ride into power. It makes me feel ashamed of my countrymen. Need I say that the English point to it and say that it is the result of democratic institutions; that they find more pleasure in it than in anything that has occurred; and that they agree with rebel papers in saying that the North will receive a heavier blow in the success of the Democracy than in any battle or event that has ever occurred?

I console myself, however, in the belief that should these men obtain the power they are seeking, they will not be so base as to produce dissension, but, once in power and their object gained, they will support the government to a successful conclusion of this rebellion.

What Mr. Hartley did in this second and self-imposed part of his mission was not only through his personal intercourse with people, but also by printing and distributing tracts to show the real issues which divided the South from the North; for it was about these things that the English had but a vague idea and were consequently most prejudiced. The following is an illustration of what Mr. Hartley did. During his stay in England he had observed the strong support which John Bright, member of Parliament for Birmingham, had given to the cause of the North. Seeing in the paper one day that Mr. Bright would speak on American affairs, Mr. Hartley determined to attend the meeting. In an article published in the "New York Times Saturday Review" on January 22, 1898, he thus gives an account of the meeting:

I was in Birmingham at the time, and seeing a notice of a meeting at the Town Hall, at which Mr. Bright was to speak on American affairs, I attended it. I was within a few feet of the platform, and the hall was crowded to overflowing. Mr. Bright commenced his speech by referring to matters in his own country, but after a while drifted to the American question and England's position.

He soon showed how he was going to treat the subject; that he was in favor of the North; but before he had given full evidence of this there was an uproar seldom heard at a meeting, and he was not allowed to proceed. He stood his ground, however, until the disturbance had ceased, then started again, with the same result, but he was not to be put down.

Standing silent, resting one hand on the table and the other in the breast of his coat, he gazed at the audience. After a while he was permitted to continue.

Mr. Bright spoke for over an hour. I listened with wonder

and admiration to his eloquent and masterly presentation of the cause for which he pleaded. It seemed impossible to present the claims of the North more forcibly. When he had finished he had his audience with him, and they cheered with the same zest as they had previously hissed. If I am not mistaken, this was the first speech that he had made in England in favor of the North, and from that time forward public sentiment began to change.

When I left the meeting that night I determined, if possible, to have the speech printed and distributed throughout England, so as to give it greater publicity and importance than it would receive at the hands of the press, which was generally hostile to the North.

Mr. Bright was the guest of the Mayor of Birmingham, and the next morning I called on him at Edgebaston, reaching there early, and while they were at breakfast. I sent in my card, making it known that I was from New York. He arose from the breakfast-table and came to me, inviting me to breakfast.

I had already breakfasted and thanked him for his kindness. I told him that I had listened to his speech the night before, probably being the only American in the hall, and had come to express my gratitude and to beg that he allow me to have it printed. After some hesitation, he consented to do so, provided I would let him correct a copy. He sent me the speech, and I had ten thousand copies struck off and distributed throughout England, where I thought they would do most good. Afterwards I had five thousand more printed, and took some of them myself to Paris and had a copy placed under the plate of every American at the Hôtel du Louvre, who were mostly from the South.

Thus was the grand, exhaustive speech of John Bright scattered over Great Britain and among the enemies of the North domiciled in Paris. I have never doubted that it contributed largely to enlighten the British public as to the real issues of the war, and in which direction their interest lay. The North, indeed the entire American people, owe a debt of gratitude to the memory of John Bright which it should never permit to perish.

With Mr. Bright, indeed, Mr. Hartley remained on friendly terms. The two were in complete accord regarding the Rebellion, and Mr. Hartley on more than one occasion thanked the Englishman for his services in helping the cause of the North in the mother country. In a letter of May 5, 1863, to Mr. Bright, he said, among other things:

> The people are firm in the determination of putting this rebellion down, and you may, my dear sir, be as positive, and speak as plainly as you can express yourself, that this cursed rebellion will be crushed, and with it slavery.

> I enclose a few articles, cut from different papers, in reply to the articles of the London "Times" about the letter of our Minister, Mr. Adams. When in Europe one would judge, from reading some of the English journals, that the people here were anxious for a quarrel with England. I find nothing of the sort except from some of our imported citizens. The masses here still cherish for England—or rather for the intelligent middle classes of England—that respect and friendship that has always existed, and I found the same attitude in England towards the intelligent American.

> I send you by this mail a copy of the "New York Times" containing an account of the movement of General Hooker. He has commenced well, and we hope he will be able to follow it up.

In April, 1863, Mr. Hartley, having accomplished the object of his mission, returned to New York. He had been away upwards of nine months, and during that time had purchased over two hundred thousand stand of arms and other equipments by which the Northern army was substantially supplied, had obtained the option from manufacturers of many thousands more, and had, in several instances, thwarted the South in their efforts to obtain aid in similar directions. He had also done much to enlighten the British nation as to the real issues of the war and to change popular sentiment. Though, of course, his task had been a difficult one, he had his reward not only in the satisfactory accomplishment of his mission, but in the hearty thanks of the War Department, and in the knowledge that he had done his country substantial service. Incidentally, it may be said that when he presented to the Secretary of War a statement of his accounts, involving the expenditure of many millions of dollars, he was complimented by the Secretary in that they were the most complete and business-like of all that had come before him during his administration, and were a model accounting of fiduciary responsibility. The following letter, written some months before his return, gives the best notion of the magnitude and the variety of his services:

BIRMINGHAM, December 24, 1862.

*Dear Sir:*

I am busy closing my books for a balance and arranging the vouchers, numbering them so as they will be readily checked. As I have said before, I have not had sufficient force in the office, being afraid to bring any outside person in for fear of collusion with the manufacturers, and for fear of information being carried outside. We have done a large business, the largest probably done within the same time by any firm in Birmingham. The only assistance I have had is Mr. Tomes and a younger brother of mine, a clergyman whom I sent for that I might have some one to rely on in an emergency. I have endeavored to manage things as economically as possible and think you will agree with me when you see my expense account.

Of the £580,000 to my credit, I have drawn about £490,000, leaving a balance of, say, £90,000 not used. The delay of the *Hammonia*, owing to an accident, prevented us from obtaining the charges until the 22d, and the fact that 390 cases Enfields, having been shut out, will have to go by the *New York* to-day from Southampton, again delays us. I had made arrangements some three weeks since to send the 69's from Antwerp with direct bill-of-lading, in case I could not dispose of them by the steamer of the 24th (to-day), for if shipped before it would have thrown out just so many cases of Enfields, the charges of which I had so as to close my accounts in time for the steamer of the 20th, but the fact is, that there is a great deal of work in balancing the books. But one pair of hands and one head can work at it. Monday we discovered an error of £288 in our favor, which Barings paid. I shall not lose an hour in sending them.

My object in writing now is to call your attention to the enclosed slips cut from the "Post," thinking they may be of service to some one.

I have not had a very agreeable task among these Englishmen. When I have had the time, and the persons warranted me in taking pains to represent our affairs at home in their true light, I have never failed to accomplish my object.

I heard Mr. Bright deliver his famous speech last Thursday night. I was so pleased with it that I called next morning at the Mayor's house to thank him, as an American, for his effort.

He received me very cordially. I desired him to allow me to have it printed in pamphlet form. Yesterday I received a letter from him, accompanied with his speech, corrected ready for the printer. I have put it in the hands of the printer, ordering one thousand to start on. This is a personal invest- ment. I have seen so much ignorance about our affairs and so much animosity, that I thought I might serve our common cause by doing something toward removing it. The effect of his speech shows itself already in the tone of the articles appearing in some of the public journals on American affairs. The paper from which the enclosed was cut has misrepresented us continually. In acknowledging the receipt of Mr. Bright's letter to-day, I wrote him that I hoped he would not remain silent so long again.

It is my intention to send my accounts, accompanied with vouchers, to the firm in New York, they to present them to the department.

My wife and family are in Paris. I intend to join them and recruit my impaired health for a time.

I remain, dear sir,
Yours very truly,
MARCELLUS HARTLEY.

P. H. WATSON, ESQ.


Mr. Hartley's patriotic services did not end here. In the spring of 1864, the Metropolitan Fair was held in New York for the purpose of raising funds for the benefit of the wounded and sick in the army and their families at home. In aid of this object he had several thousand copies of the "Philanthropic Results of the War," which he had prepared on his return from Europe, for gratu- itous circulation, bound and presented to the Fair as his contribution. This small book of one hundred and sixty pages is a clear and glowing account of the origin and work of the Sanitary and Christian Commissions and of the various other ways in which patriotic men and women furthered the cause of freedom and alleviated the misery brought to soldier and civilian alike by the magnitude of the struggle. The orderly and systematic account of the amount of money, over $212,000,000, raised by state and private charity in this honorable service is characteristic of Mr. Hartley, but not more so than the tales of self-sacrifice and devotion with which the volume teems, nor than the generous and hopeful spirit of patriotism which animates the whole. Not only did the book net several thousand dollars to the income of the Fair, but Mr. Hartley sent hundreds of copies to similar fairs in other parts of the country. Several went to England. "I should like it," he said in a letter to Mr. Bright of April 13, 1864, "if the facts in the little book were given to the English people. It would be of interest to them, and would show that we were more like the English in spirit than they give us credit for."

Shortly after his return from Europe, Mr. Hartley resumed his old position in the firm of Schuyler, Hartley, and Graham. He found the business largely extended and very prosperous. Aided by his experience it increased in the next few years to even larger proportions. But the history of that increase is important enough to be treated in a separate chapter.

## VI

### *Expansion of Business after the Civil War*
### *(1864–1888)*

THE Civil War had given Mr. Hartley exceptional
opportunities to become acquainted with the manufacture of arms and ammunition all over the world. This
experience was of inestimable value to him in succeeding years. Furthermore, his firm had been prosperous
during the period, and the stimulus which the war gave
to inventions and improvements in the manufacture of
arms enabled him to employ his accumulated capital to
great advantage. During the years that followed he
acquired much wealth, but it was gained in a solid and
steady way; for his fortunes were based entirely upon
industrial success, and his enterprises were mainly the
creation of his sagacity and sound judgment. Indeed
his business career from beginning to end was an example of the conception, the building up, and the constant
watching of substantial industries which gave to thousands of people regular employment, and made many
families prosperous and successful. This expansion of
his business has four main aspects.

The first of these was the opportunity afforded by the
invention of the breech-loading rifle. Breech-loading

rifles had been used early in the century, but until within
a few years before the outbreak of the Civil War without
much success.    The men in America to do most for the
perfecting of these arms were perhaps the Remingtons,
from whose works in the town of Ilion, New York, were
turned out during the Civil War and in after years many
rifles bearing the famous name.    With the introduction
of the breech-loading rifle arose the question of ammunition, and it was in the perfecting, not so much of the
idea of the weapon, as of the facility, speed, regularity,
and uniformity of production, that Mr. Hartley saw his
first great opportunity to establish an excellent business.
"There is no country," he wrote to Anson Burlingame,
February 8, 1866, "that can compete with us in breech-
loading arms.    It is now the universally acknowledged
principle.    This you know, and if they [the Chinese] are
to have arms, they should have the most approved."
Indeed, he had had the idea of suitable ammunition long
in mind; it had come to him as early as the year 1855,
while a clerk in the employ of Tomes.    When on one
of his trips to the West, a chance acquaintance, learning
that Mr. Hartley was interested in guns, showed him a
roughly made metallic shell in which the charge for a
gun could be inclosed.    Mr. Hartley at once perceived
the value of the idea, but, without expressing more than
an ordinary interest in it, asked his fellow-traveler to
give him the shell.    That souvenir led, some years later,
to the establishment of the Union Metallic Cartridge

Company, the most successful and profitable of the manufacturing interests in which Mr. Hartley was engaged. The idea both of the breech-loading rifle and of the metallic cartridge was, as has been said, an old one; Mr. Hartley's contribution to the art of warfare consisted of the effectual and economical manufacture, on a large scale, of the first successful metallic cartridge ever made and adopted, practically, throughout the world.

Mr. Hartley could not put his idea into effect, however, until after the close of the Civil War. That plan his work for the United States Government prevented, and, moreover, it was the war itself, and the increased demand for arms after it, that gave him the opportunity that he desired. Then, on investigation, he found that only a few factories in the East had attempted the manufacture of metallic cartridges, but without success in any large or effectual way. Discouraged, they had finally abandoned their work, and had offered their plants and patents for sale. Of these the Crittenden and Tibbals Manufacturing Company of South Coventry, Connecticut, and that of C. D. Leet of Springfield, Massachusetts, were bought by Mr. Hartley's firm. The firm had, previously, in September, 1865, purchased a large tract of land, at Bridgeport, for the site of a plant; and on the ninth of August, 1867, incorporated the Union Metallic Cartridge Company under the laws of the State of Connecticut. The corporation consisted, in addition to Mr. Schuyler, Mr. Hartley, and Mr. Graham, of Mr.

Charles H. Pond, who was made the president of the company, and Mr. Robert J. White, who was chosen secretary and treasurer.

For a time the firm manufactured cartridges, percussion-caps, and shot-guns, but soon gave up the manufacture of the last. The first cartridges, though improvements on the existing models, were comparatively crude. At the outset only rim-fire cartridges were made, but, on the coming in of the center-fire system, the company proceeded at once to manufacture these also. The improvements which the firm made in early forms of the cartridge were due chiefly to the ingenuity and mechanical skill of Mr. A. C. Hobbs, superintendent of the works until his death in 1891, and by his experiments excellent cartridges were made to meet the requirements of the various models of breech-loading rifles. The company also manufactured cartridges under the patents of Hiram Berdan and other successful inventors, and as a result received large orders from many of the European governments for suitable and effective ammunition. Consequently, the business increased very rapidly, until, from the little more than an acre of floor space originally required, there are to-day no less than ten acres devoted to the manufacture of all kinds of fixed ammunition, from the smallest percussion-cap to large six-inch cases. For upward of twenty years the development of this business devolved mainly upon Mr. Hartley, who, on the death of his partners, Mr. Schuyler and Mr. Graham, bought their interests and continued at the head of the business until the time of his death. This was the greatest of all Mr. Hartley's enterprises.

The second enterprise of Mr. Hartley during this period was the establishment in February, 1878, of the Bridgeport Gun Implement Company. Prior to that year appliances for sportsmen's use, such as rods, cleaners, extractors, powder-measures, and reloading tools, had been made in this country only in small quantity. The varieties, too, were limited to the requirements of certain manufacturers of firearms, and consequently there was a considerable monopoly in the business. At that time, also, the sale of factory-loaded paper shot shells was a thing unknown, and the metal shells then used had to be recharged by sportsmen, as best they could, with a crude and clumsy yet expensive outfit imported from Europe. At this factory, Mr. Hartley, as in the case of rifles, entered upon the manufacture of a line of goods that came into use with the passing of the old muzzle-loading shot-gun. The business rapidly increased, more buildings became necessary, and the firm manufactured articles not only in firearms and shells, but in general sporting goods as well.

Closely connected with the Bridgeport Gun Implement Company was Mr. Hartley's interest in electricity, which was then becoming known as an illuminant and source of power. Mr. Hartley was quick to foresee

its possibilities and predicted its success. Desiring, however, to produce better apparatus than the dynamos
then in use, and to make an incandescent lamp at once
serviceable and cheap, he had a laboratory fitted up at
the works in Bridgeport and employed Mr. Hiram
Maxim, the well-known inventor, to experiment with
dynamos and various forms of lamps, and the company
itself took contracts for the manufacture of these commodities. Mr. Maxim was successful in producing an
economical article, but had been slightly outstripped
in the race by Mr. Edison. Encouraged, however, by
the success of the experiment, Mr. Hartley determined
to pursue the business considerably further. Having
secured the patents of Mr. Maxim, Mr. Farmer, Mr.
Weston, and other inventors, he determined to establish
in New York a company to manufacture electrical apparatus and to build plants for the transmission of power.
The company was organized with a capital of $300,000,
which was subsequently increased to $1,500,000. Sub-
companies of the United States Electric Lighting Company, as it was called, were also established in many
of our large cities, and there seemed to be every pros-
pect of success. The opposition, however, arising from
the skepticism of the public, the jealousy of rich gas
companies, the competition of rivals, the heavy expenses
incident to the introduction of all new enterprises,
and much costly litigation for the defending of its
patents, combined to retard the progress of the com-

pany. Mr. Hartley, though confident of ultimate success, thought best to sell the whole concern to Mr. George Westinghouse, who had recently established the Westinghouse Electric and Manufacturing Company, and in this Mr. Hartley's company was merged. Mr. Hartley and his associates, however, retained their interest in the new corporation, and Mr. Hartley accepted the vice-presidency of it. The success of the company was phenomenal. Beyond this merely financial question, the success of Mr. Hartley's work meant the practical demonstration of the superiority of the so-called alternating electric current system, which when first started by Mr. Hartley was bitterly opposed by other companies using the direct electric current system then in vogue.

The fourth and last enterprise to which Mr. Hartley gave his chief attention was the Remington Arms Company of Ilion, New York, of which mention has been made in the beginning of this chapter. During the Civil War, and at the time of the Franco-Prussian War, the Remington Arms Company had been exceedingly prosperous, but in the comparatively peaceful times after those conflicts the diminution of their business compelled them to go into other forms of manufacture than that in which they had originally engaged. These enterprises had not been successful; in March, 1888, the plant was sold at auction by the receivers, in whose hands it had been for some years. Mr. Hartley, in connection with the Winchester Arms Company, bought the entire plant

AT FORTY-FIVE YEARS OF AGE

and reorganized the company under the name of the Remington Arms Company. Later on his firm purchased the interest which the Winchester Repeating Arms Company had in the Remington Arms Company and became sole owners. On the death of Mr. Graham the whole property passed into the hands of Mr. Hartley.

Meanwhile the original business of Mr. Hartley's firm continued. The Civil War, as we have seen, helped it much. So, too, the Franco-Prussian War and the Russo-Turkish War brought additional business to it. That partnership was broken in the year 1875 by the retirement of Mr. Schuyler, and in 1899 by the death of Mr. Graham. No new members were added; and the business in April, 1900, was incorporated under the name of the M. Hartley Company.

Such were the chief business interests of Mr. Hartley's life. They showed admirably the various lines of work which occupied him. It was a life devoted to sound and epoch-making industrial enterprises; steady, stable, successful.

the city, he would, rain or shine, mount his horse, nor was he satisfied until he had ridden ten or fifteen miles. It is doubtful whether within that radius he did not, at one time or other, cover every accessible rod of road. Altogether he did an immense amount of riding; indeed, he missed few days in the entire twelvemonth. His most usual route, especially toward the end of his life, was along the shady road of Llewellyn Park to Montclair, and thence home by the top of the mountain. From here he could see the sun as it sank behind the range of hills to the west, while to the east would break out the myriads of electric lights in New York and the smaller towns. To the south, the view from his place extended to the Narrows: on a clear day he could see the shore of Long Island. To the north, over the marshes of the Passaic and the Hackensack, his eye rested on the green, woody back of the Palisades.

Mr. Hartley's habits were most simple. On coming in from his ride, he would prepare for his dinner, and after that would smoke and read the evening papers or some historical or biographical work. Rarely did he sit up beyond half-past ten, and to this simple, quiet, methodical life can be ascribed the remarkably good health which he enjoyed to the close of his days. On Sunday only did he vary from this regularity. Then he attended service at the St. Cloud Presbyterian Church, a pretty ivy-covered stone chapel, erected by the summer residents on the mountain to provide a

suitable place for Dr. Adams to continue the summer
services which he had begun in his study. The chapel
was about a mile distant from Mr. Hartley's home;
thither and back he walked, no matter what the weather
might be.

The society which Mr. Hartley found in this little
community was to him most congenial; it consisted of
neighbors with whom he stood upon terms of delightful intimacy. They were the Rev. Dr. Adams, General Randolph B. Marcy, General George B. McClellan,
George Hecker, Dr. E. E. Marcy, John Crosby Brown,
Eugene Delano, and Douglas Robinson. Frequently
on summer evenings might be seen gathered together
on the piazza of one of the summer homes Dr. Adams,
General Marcy, General McClellan, Mr. Brown, Mr.
Delano, and Mr. Hartley, with the members of their
families, engaged in friendly chat. The army had the
upper hand, because richer in interest and anecdote.
General Marcy would, in his entertaining way, tell some
exciting tales of his Indian campaigns, of his fierce en-
counters with and hair-breadth escapes from grizzly
bears in the Rocky Mountains; General McClellan,
more reticent until warmed up, would relate incidents and
anecdotes of his long and varied experience in army
life; while the genial, courtly Dr. Adams, as a fit ending,
would conclude with some amusing episode of his cleri-
cal career.

Of those who frequently accompanied Mr. Hartley,

not only upon his walks to and from church but also in the long rambles which he delighted to take among the woods and over the hills, General Randolph B. Marcy was the most constant companion. The two had a great affection for each other. General Marcy was a retired officer of the regular army; he had served with distinction in the Mexican War, had explored the Red River country, and had fought through the Rebellion. His genial manners, the richness and variety of his experiences, and the fact that, notwithstanding his advanced years, he was a good pedestrian and a charming companion, made him especially congenial to Mr. Hartley. Often the latter would tell how much he missed General Marcy at his death, and he sometimes related a touching incident which happened at the funeral. It was to the effect that General Sherman, who, though old and enfeebled, was present, stepped forward and kissed his dead friend, saying, " Good-by, my dear old comrade; I shall soon be with you."

When, however, summer advanced and the heat became oppressive, Mr. Hartley would, with his family, leave the Orange Mountains for cooler places. Of these Long Branch was the most convenient resort during the busy days of the Civil War, for it enabled him to reach his business easily. With the more leisurely period which followed the war, he would go to a greater distance from the city, and for some years made it his custom to spend a few weeks of each summer at Saratoga. Here, besides the benefit which he received from the complete change of air, he had the pleasure of meeting many old friends, among whom were Isaac N. Phelps, James Brown, Dr. John T. Metcalf, and Henry A. Hurlbut. Here, too, he saw many foreigners whom he knew in a business or social way and whose company he enjoyed.

In 1882 he gave up Saratoga for the Catskills. Here he did much walking, and from his excellent knowledge of the country he frequently became the guide of his companions through the tortuous paths among the mountains. Among his companions in these tramps were Justice Strong and Mr. Alexander Brown. In the Catskills, however, he missed his favorite pastimes of bathing, riding, and driving, and consequently the next season he went to Southampton, Long Island, where the excellent roads and invigorating surf enabled him to indulge to the fullest extent in his favorite exercises. At Southampton his companion was Dr. Markoe, his neighbor in the city. They would go bathing together nearly every day, and would often amuse themselves in the pleasant sport of shooting at a target. Dr. Markoe was perhaps his closest friend; their intimacy was without reserve. Although Dr. Markoe was Mr. Hartley's senior by many years, yet the freshness of his spirit, the geniality of his disposition, and their similar tastes made them such delightful companions to each other that their friendship continued until the death of Dr. Markoe.

After 1895 Mr. Hartley abandoned his yearly visits

to Southampton, owing to the death of his daughter, Grace Hartley Stokes, and his granddaughter, Emma Hartley Stokes, who had been with him at that place. The associations became so painful that he was unable to return. Succeeding summers, accordingly, he spent at Simsbury and Norfolk, Connecticut, where his fondness for good riding was fully satisfied. He also made several visits to Canada, and had much pleasure in showing his family the interesting places there. From a driving trip that he and his family took in the White Mountains he derived an enjoyment which he was never tired of recalling. The variety of these excursions was a means of diversion and real refreshment to his spirit.

During the last three summers of his life he took trips successively to Montreal and Quebec, the Thousand Islands, and Bar Harbor. These he made with his friend, Mr. John A. Browning, and his grandson, and, according to the accounts of his companions, Mr. Hartley on these occasions exchanged the cares of his business for genuine relaxation. His playful remarks constantly kept his companions in his own mirthful humor. The usual programme was a walk in the morning through the village where they happened to be; their amusement lay in the various articles or books in the stores and the different types of people that they met. In the afternoon a horseback ride was usual. It was not infrequent for Mr. Hartley to be caught in a rainstorm several miles from home and to ride back thoroughly drenched. In all these things he found diversion. He seemed to particularly enjoy the month he spent at Bar Harbor during his last summer.

The following little story, told by one of Mr. Hartley's fellow-travelers, is characteristic:

"We started on Sunday morning for a certain church. On arriving there we found the building overcrowded because of a visiting clergyman, and we accordingly entered a simple little chapel farther on. We all agreed that the sermon there was excellent, although some of its points did not harmonize with Mr. Hartley's ideas of orthodoxy. During the discussion which followed, Mr. Hartley, after a brief interval of silence, suddenly exclaimed: 'Life is a mystery, anyhow. The only thing to do is to play trumps all the time.' 'What are trumps?' asked one of the three. 'Hearts,' he said instantly, and looked earnestly and inquisitively into the eyes of his questioner."

All in all, Mr. Hartley's conception of a vacation was that in it one should get himself into such condition that he could derive enjoyment from his work. Whereas many workers go on the principle of getting enjoyment in their vacation after hard work in their regular occupation, Mr. Hartley reversed the process. His idea was "get your fun from your work."

As has been hinted in the preceding paragraphs, the pleasant life of Mr. Hartley was interrupted, on more than one occasion, by the greatest sorrow which mankind has to bear—the loss of children. On May 6, 1880, his eldest daughter, Emma, was married to Mr. Norman White Dodge. In anticipation of their marriage,

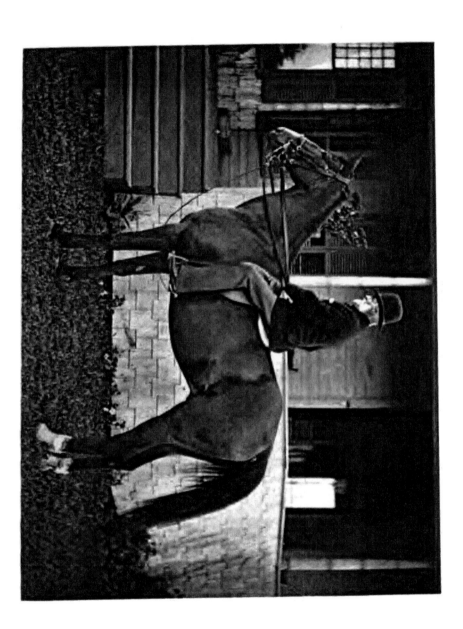

Mr. Hartley had bought the house in Thirty-seventh Street which adjoins his own on Madison Avenue, and had had it reconstructed and connected with his own. Here Mrs. Dodge went to live, and her nearness to her father was always a source of great joy to him. In her death, however, which occurred the third of March, 1881, Mr. Hartley sustained the great affliction of his life. It was, since the death of his infant daughter, his first bereavement, and the loss came almost without warning. Crushing though the blow was to him, the fortitude with which Mr. Hartley bore up under the loss of this beloved daughter was a source of wonder to those who knew what an idol she had been to him. He found consolation in the son who took his grandfather's name, and to him Mr. Hartley's affection was transferred. Indeed, on no one did he lavish more love and tenderness than on Marcellus Hartley Dodge. The year was one of a double sorrow: almost in the hour of his daughter's death, his venerable and beloved father ended his long career of usefulness.

The following year, on the twenty-seventh of November, 1882, one of his twin daughters, Grace, was married to Mr. James Stokes. Mr. Hartley had bought for her a country home next his own on the Orange Mountains, and since Mr. Stokes was also a near neighbor in the city, Mr. Hartley was enabled to see his daughter very frequently. On December 20, 1884, a daughter was born to Mrs. Stokes.

This child, Emma Hartley Stokes, was, for her years, remarkably clever and mature, and of very winning ways. At the age of eleven, however, she was taken away. There had been a son, Marcellus Hartley Stokes, younger than the girl, but he had died at the age of eighteen months; and the death of this only daughter, depriving Mrs. Stokes of both her children, was more than she could bear. On Easter morning, 1896, she died suddenly, but a few months after her daughter. Mr. Hartley suffered deepest anguish of spirit at this second double bereavement. No affliction could have been more sad and poignant, but he received it with that calm resignation which came from well-grounded faith in his religion, and which enabled him to say, " The Lord gave and the Lord hath taken away; blessed be the name of the Lord."

There now remained in Mr. Hartley's family the twin sister of Mrs. Stokes and his grandson. On the 30th of June, 1892, this daughter, Helen, was married to Mr. George Walker Jenkins. There are two daughters, Helen Hartley Jenkins and Grace Hartley Jenkins.

# VIII

## *Last Years (1888–1902)*

WITH the buying of the Remington Arms Company in 1888, and the placing of that interest on a substantial basis, the main line of Mr. Hartley's business enterprises was completed, and what remained for him to do was chiefly the overseeing of his various property. He was then sixty-one years of age, and had consequently reached the time when many men are willing, so far as possible, to retire and repose under well-earned laurels. With Mr. Hartley the case was different. Up to the time of his death, he continued to be actively employed in making solid and in broadening his industries, and he also took a hand in many new affairs. He gave much time and advice to other business and to worthy charity, and the years were of intense and ceaseless activity.

The cause of this activity is not far to seek. Doubtless it may be partly found in the fact that Mr. Hartley's wide experience and proved sagacity made him an invaluable counselor to friends whose requests he was too good-natured to refuse; but those who have followed his life during the decade of 1880–1890 will also perceive that he was then passing through a critical stage

temperamentally.   Up to 1881 his life had been one of
constant success and growing triumph.   In that year
the death of his daughter smote him so sorely that his
best hope of forgetfulness lay in hard work.   The following deaths in his family urged him in the same direction.   Hence, in part at least, came the eagerness with
which he welcomed new opportunities to occupy his
energy, and hence, perhaps, it was that when he died
he died suddenly and in the harness.

The man who, probably, did most to save Mr. Hartley
from dwelling too much upon his sorrow was the late
Henry Baldwin Hyde, president of the Equitable Life
Assurance Society.   The two men had become acquainted not far from the time of Emma Hartley's death.
Through Mr. Hyde, Mr. Hartley became a director in
the Equitable and later in many of the companies controlled by that Society.   The fact that Mr. Hartley was
a member of the Executive Committee of the Equitable
and for some time chairman of it brought him into frequent contact with Mr. Hyde; they regularly met each
other three times a week and often every day to talk
over the business of the Society.   One of the results
was the forming of a close friendship, which was pecu-
liarly striking because of the confidence each gave to
the other, and the regard shown by each for the soundness of the other's judgment.   That was the beginning
of a long series of offices of trust into which Mr. Hartley
entered outside his own manufacturing concerns, and

which gave his great energy constant occupation. It must not, of course, be inferred from what has been said that Mr. Hartley was ever in danger of yielding to morbid depression over his sorrow; his reason was too clear and firmly seated for any such catastrophe; he was always completely master of himself. What he was enabled to do through the help of his friend was, however, to find serious and useful forms of distraction, and it was in such boards of deliberation that his experience and judgment were invaluable.

It is impossible to write of this period of Mr. Hartley's life without speaking of a gentleman who was on several boards of directors with him. With no one did Mr. Hartley cherish a closer intimacy than with William A. Wheelock. It seems right to say that to him Mr. Hartley gave his complete confidence, and derived unbounded pleasure from a friendship extending over nearly half a century.

It is unnecessary to give a complete list of the various corporations with which Mr. Hartley was connected during the last years of his life, and of which he was a director. Among them were the Manhattan Railroad Company, the Western, Lincoln, and German-American National Banks, the Mercantile Trust Company, the Fifth Avenue Trust Company, the American District Telegraph Company, the Audit Company, the American Surety Company, and, finally, the International Banking Corporation. In the first two and the last two of these he was on the Executive Committee. These various institutions required his constant attention, some daily and others weekly, and he was rarely missing from their meetings. He had also the charge of several estates which claimed his thoughtful care and large amounts of his time. How he managed to perform all these various duties was a source of wonder to those familiar with his business life, but the reason has been stated above. Whatever he did, he did without apparent strain and with little perturbation.

Such offices as these frequently fall to the lot of successful and prominent business men. By them these positions are regarded partly in the light of honorary rewards for their sagacity and partly as a public duty imposed upon them by the ideals of business. Such posts may be looked upon as semi-charities. The description may certainly be applied to Mr. Hartley's work in reinvigorating the "New York Times," wherein he did the community a notable service in preventing that paper from lapsing from the respectable and intelligent paper that it always had been into a sensational sheet. It was at a time when, in the words of the present proprietor, "the necessity of conducting newspapers along sensational lines had almost grown into a superstition among the journalists of this country." The desire of the management, however, was that the paper should remain true to the respectable ideal that it had always had. Furthermore, they wished, if possible, to reduce the price to one cent, not only as a business policy, but that

FROM LAST PHOTOGRAPH

the paper might be within the reach of the poorer classes at the same price as the cheap sensational journals. The question was one of finance, since considerable loss would be sustained in making the venture. The possibilities of the move impressed Mr. Hartley and appealed to his civic sense; he came forward with an offer to advance the money necessary to make the change, and to assume any deficiency that there might be until such time as the publisher could place the sheet on a self-sustaining basis. The venture proved to be completely successful. The circulation and the advertising patronage rapidly increased, and before long the paper not only paid expenses, but yielded a large profit. Mr. Hartley's disinterestedness is shown in the fact that, again to quote the present proprietor of the paper, he "was for six years a member of the Board of Directors of the 'New York Times' Company, simply holding a qualifying share in the company. Had he owned a large block of stock, he could not have been more useful with his advice or helpful with his money. He never at any time tried to influence the general policy of the newspaper, and never asked any special consideration for himself, his friends, or any interest he and they represented." This is but an example of the kind of philanthropy which Mr. Hartley frequently practised. It was of that valuable sort of charity which puts worthy business enterprises on a solid and paying basis, and in so doing confers a substantial and honorable gift upon all members of a community.

Mr. Hartley, however, was charitable in the more strict sense of the word. Perhaps his most conspicuous service was what he did for the support of the Hartley House. Early in the year 1897 an industrial settlement was opened at 413 West Forty-sixth Street by the Association for Improving the Condition of the Poor, an institution which his father had been instrumental in founding. In memory of Robert Milham Hartley the Association had named the new settlement Hartley House. In it Mr. Hartley took keen interest and pleasure. He soon purchased the building which the settlement was occupying and presented it to the Association. It happened that his daughter, Mrs. James Stokes, had bequeathed a sum of money to found a kindergarten. Mr. Hartley added largely to this fund, and the Emma Hartley Stokes Kindergarten, thus founded and endowed, was placed in the Hartley House. Subsequently, Mr. Hartley, to enlarge the work of the settlement, bought two more buildings and added a large gymnasium. He not only contributed much money to the support of the settlement, but he made its interests his own, and served on its Board of Directors until his death.

The last and perhaps the most conspicuous activity of any sort was the interest he took in the International Banking Corporation, of which he was president. This concern occupied much of his time and thought in the months preceding his death, which occurred on the afternoon of January 8, 1902. For a few days previous he had been complaining of indigestion, but, since his health had always been good and he had scarcely ever been confined at home, he thought little of the matter. On the morning of the sad occurrence he left his house in his usual cheerful humor and drove to his office, where he was engaged during the morning. Then he attended a meeting of the Executive Committee of the Equitable Life Assurance Society, took lunch with one of his most valued friends, Mr. James W. Alexander, and afterwards went to a meeting of the Executive Committee of the American Surety Company. His colleagues were seated about the long table of the room. With them he chatted gaily for a moment, but presently became silent. It was then noticed that his head was drooping lower and lower on his chest. To a question whether he felt faint he could make no reply; his head fell forward, and in an instant, with the arms of Mr. Smith about him and his hand clasped in Mr. Wheelock's, surrounded by friends and business associates, Marcellus Hartley passed away.

His funeral took place on the following Saturday from the Madison Square Presbyterian Church, whence other members of his family had been carried for burial. In the absence of his pastor, Dr. Charles H. Parkhurst, Bishop Potter and the Rev. Dr. Roderick Terry conducted the service. The pall-bearers were his friends and associates in business. They were William A. Wheelock, Levi P. Morton, D. Willis James, Anson Phelps Stokes, Eugene Delano, James W. Alexander, Andrew Carnegie, James H. Hyde, John A. Stewart, William E. Dodge, R. Fulton Cutting, George Westinghouse, General Louis Fitzgerald, General Thomas C. Eckert, Russell Sage, General Thomas H. Hubbard, George W. Hebard, and Valentine P. Snyder. Most of these friends have written tributes to Mr. Hartley's life and character; what they have said, together with some editorial comments, will be found at the end of this volume. Mr. Hartley was buried at Greenwood. He is survived by his widow, his daughter, and his three grandchildren.

# IX

## *Character*

IT remains to make a general statement of the personal traits, the character, the ideals, and the business principles of Mr. Hartley. Physically Mr. Hartley was below the ordinary height and was rather light of frame. His complexion was fair, his eyes grayish blue and of unusual penetration, his features clear-cut and firm, and his whole expression was one of keenness, composure, and tenderness. His step was vigorous, though slow and measured, and all his movements expressed controlled energy. He bore himself with dignity, and his demeanor was one of quiet self-respect.

By temperament and training Mr. Hartley was, in the best sense of the word, practical. From the account of his interests given in the preceding pages, it is evident that he was wholly alive to the working value of an idea. For theorizing and for pure speculation he had no liking, but his mind was constantly occupied with the putting into practice of some idea which would furnish people with commodities of substantial value, and which would directly increase their comfort and convenience. " I am," he wrote in 1886, " still hard at work. It would be easy for me to retire in one sense, but I sincerely believe a man is better off hard at work. I believe the true way to benefit mankind and those who make up your world is to keep them employed, developing interests, giving them a chance to live, putting your money into their enterprises. Though they are not always successful, still you give a living to many families." His temperament may, therefore, be described as active, and his training had, from his first entry into business, been of the sort to foster rather than to repress what was the most striking quality of his intellect—his ability to see the practical bearings of whatever he applied his mind to. In the hundreds of business letters which he wrote the main idea seems to be: "This thing will work" or "This thing will not work."

Expressed rather more profoundly, the idea which dominated Mr. Hartley's activity was that life is a serious business, not an affair merely of pleasure and sentiment. For romance and sentimentality, those forces which urge a man to seek his joy in what is not rather than what is, which lead him to override and trample on the facts of the world, and at their best raise him to astounding heights of individuality, Mr. Hartley had little liking. He read the letters of life clearly, swiftly, and without evasion. There is in some of his later personal correspondence a hint of a singularly simple and straightforward view of the world. Life is an affair of plain daily duties, of making the best of opportunities, of honest endeavor, of ceaseless, often sad, striving. We are placed in this world, the note is, not for our earthly pleasure, but, under the guiding hand of Providence, for our eternal honor. To its decrees we must bow. "I wish I could say or do something to break the blow," he wrote to a friend, "but it is useless. It is beyond all human power. We take a different view of life after such an event; our hold is shaken; we begin to look to the future, and after a while we have more on the other side than on this. This is the way Providence has of dealing; we must accept it and cannot alter it, and after a while would not, if we could." So it was that Mr. Hartley's life was spent in constant labor, untouched by idleness and untainted by depression.

Such views are not uncommon. What, however, distinguished Mr. Hartley from the great majority of his serious fellow-men was the union of this sober philosophy with great clearness and firmness of intellect. He saw his facts clearly and readily, down to the minute details. Nothing, perhaps, in the history of his mind is more striking than the fact that he knew the small things of his business, and never regarded them as unworthy of his notice. Facts, details, minutiæ were to him ever present, and it is amazing to note the number and variety of those facts over which his eye swiftly and surely ranged.

It must not, however, be imagined that Mr. Hartley's mind busied itself simply with these facts as facts. On the contrary, as has been hinted above, he always had large ends in view, and held to principles of which details were but the working out and to which they were subservient. His mind was imaginative, not in the sense that he combined the details of life into large and generous pictures, but for the reason that he saw the bearing of every detail and could make it leap and spring into new combinations with other details, from which emerged new establishments and fruitful enterprises.

Nor should it be supposed that the matter-of-fact quality of Mr. Hartley's intellect obliterated the gentler side of his nature or allowed it to suffer from neglect. The clearness of mind which always distinguished him did, indeed, carry with it a prevailing honesty, a hatred of sham, fraud, and dissimulation, which not infrequently led to severity of manner. By disposition, however, he was kind and benevolent. He wanted other people to do what he could do, to succeed as he had succeeded, and he helped many with sagacious counsel. Of his kindness there is no better example than the letters of advice which he not infrequently wrote to people who were in hard straits. From his vast acquaintance with practical affairs he mapped out a detailed plan of con- duct for them to pursue if they wished to regain their place in the world. Some of the letters are marvelously wise and helpful.

In all such letters of advice the main idea, which was worked into a wealth of detail, was self-control. In preaching this doctrine, Mr. Hartley did no more than he himself practised. Restraint was a dominant quality of his intellect. In trying and distressing circumstances he always had perfect control of himself. This seeming lack of sensibility was in no respect due to hardness of heart or to an unsympathetic nature; on the contrary, he was the kindest of men. It was but the expression of a temperament distinguished for the clearness with which it read facts and for its power of self-suppression. Mr. Hartley always submitted patiently to the inevitable. This self-control enabled him to pursue his schemes without impatience, to deny himself when a good cause could be advanced, to be systematic, perseverant, steadfast. It led him to see the folly of display and extravagance, and kept him free from affectation.

Simplicity was a striking trait of his character. He was not in the least austere, and what he wanted he usually got; but for show, as such, he had no taste. His amusements were few and wholesome. Horseback riding, walking, surf-bathing, target-shooting, billiards, and the like, were his favorite recreations. Public speaking and debate were always a source of great delight to him, and to gratify his pleasure in them he would put himself to inconvenience. He stayed much at home, and here he took great pleasure in the society of his family, in occasional games of cards with them, and not seldom in reading. His reading was confined chiefly to standard books, though he not infrequently took up novels. Biography and history he liked very much, and Napoleon was perhaps his especial favorite.

Mr. Hartley's simplicity and self-control made him rather formal in his address toward people, and may have caused him to be somewhat reserved in his friendships. He had very many friends, in business and out; but, like most clear men, few intimate ones to whom he gave his confidence. To those in whom he had faith, no man was more loyal; but he was naturally slow to forget a betrayal of his trust. Truthfulness he loved, and next to this he believed in order, punctuality, and method; these things he demanded from his employees and associates. Of all these virtues he was himself an exemplar, and they were the result of this same clear-sighted self-control.

In politics, Mr. Hartley may best be described as a patriotic American. The earliest recollection we have of his beliefs was when, as a lad visiting his grandfather at Bayside, it pleased him to call himself a Democrat, although he was too young to know the meaning of the term. In jest, his grandfather used to name him "General," after General Jackson, the popular hero of the day. When in his teens and somewhat familiar with politics, he became an ardent Whig and a great admirer of Henry Clay. On one of his trips West, in the early fifties, he called upon that distinguished statesman at the quiet shades of Ashland, Kentucky, and he would frequently relate with great zest the cordial reception he received. He often told of Clay's charm of manner, the soundness of his views, and his wonderful personal magnetism. The impression was never effaced from his mind. It is safe to say that the principles for which Clay stood always remained with Mr. Hartley.

His political beliefs, however, though constant, express themselves in adherence to different movements. On the founding of the Know-Nothing party in 1853, on the principle that America should really mean the Union of the States, with no North, no South, no East, and no West, without sectarianism in legislation or religion and without the too eager assimilation of foreigners into the body politic, Mr. Hartley gave it his support. He soon perceived, however, that the country was large enough and elastic enough to take in all who come, and, indeed, the speedy disruption of the Know-Nothing party proved his political sagacity. Then he turned to the newly risen offspring of the Whigs, the Republican party, which was formed at the opening of the Civil War, and to this he gave his earnest support until the time of his death. But he was never so wedded to party as to be subservient to its dogmas when, in his judgment, its principles were being sacrificed to advance the personal ambition of men. His knowledge of human nature enabled him quickly to discover the motives of men, and he never hesitated to oppose any selfish policy which was undermining public interest.

Mr. Hartley never held public office, though often

urged by his friends to do so. He was too busy in prosecuting his various enterprises to pay attention to the administration of public affairs. He contented himself with advising party leaders, and would contribute money whenever necessary to maintain party organization. The only exception to his purely private career was his course during the Civil War, when, as we have seen, he devoted his time and knowledge to the aid of the Government. The office, however, was in no sense a political one.

The temperament which dominated Mr. Hartley is in no way better seen than in his religion. Here his convictions were strong; though never forced upon others, they were maintained in firmness and simplicity. In manhood he united with the Madison Square Presbyterian Church, and remained faithful to it during his life. One of his chief delights, after having heard a sermon that especially pleased him, was to have it printed and distributed. In this way, particularly to a clergyman doing his duty in a sequestered church, would he show his appreciation. His regard for the Sabbath was strong; his usual diversion on this day was a long, quiet walk in the town or country.

It remains to say a few words of Mr. Hartley's business methods. His business was, of course, the main issue of his life, and for that reason the conduct of it merits special attention. In general, it was carried on with foresight, wisdom, and courage. No man's judgment was regarded as sounder or of more value by his associates in the many industrial and financial dealings which he had with them. He frequently aided them to overcome difficulties and to meet emergencies. His clear, practical, and judicial mind, fortified by over half a century of experience among men, made him in times of doubt and perplexity an invaluable friend and counselor. More than one instance is known of how Mr. Hartley helped financial institutions in trying crises. In all such cases his aid was timely and his foresight justified by the outcome.

In Mr. Hartley's business methods individuality was perhaps the chief characteristic. His personality was never obscured. His will dominated every department and irradiated the diversities of his complex affairs. To the large mass of employees he was somewhat exacting, but his manner was always kindly. He would brook no assumption on their part, but was always glad to have their views; and if they presented anything that appeared to his judgment better than his own, he would gratefully adopt it. Shirking he never permitted. The same industry and attention to business which he observed for himself he expected from all employees. His favorite formula of qualification for an employee was tact, push, and principle. Without tact and push, he argued, a man of principle may be good for many things, but not for business; and without principle all the tact and push in the world may come only to evil.

The presence of Mr. Hartley's will in his business is well illustrated by the anecdote told by a man who was twenty-five years in his employ. " In the early days of my acquaintance with Mr. Hartley, I once had occasion to dictate a letter in his presence to send to a dealer who had treated us unfairly. My letter started as follows: 'We are surprised at the position you take.' Mr. Hartley stopped me with a terse remark: 'Don't write that, young man, and as long as you are in my employ don't allow yourself to be surprised at anything. Just take people as you find them. When you have been in business as long as I have, nothing people do will surprise you. Nothing ever surprises me. Remember, you are not surprised now; they have done just what you expected rascals would do. Begin that letter over again!'" It must be added that the same writer speaks of the pleasure it was to be associated with Mr. Hartley, of the "many kindly admonitions fitly spoken in relation to business matters" which have "since served him well in times of emergency." The training received under Mr. Hartley was evidently excellent.

Mr. Hartley could get along admirably with men. The large number of old employees in his offices and factories speaks eloquently for his dealings with those under him. The same general observation is true in his relations to the members of his firm. When, in 1876, Mr. Schuyler retired, his interest was purchased by his partners and the firm name became Hartley and

Graham; shortly after the death of Mr. Graham in December, 1899, the business was incorporated as the M. Hartley Company. These were the only changes. Throughout his life, Mr. Hartley's relations with his partners were always pleasant. This was due to the fact that, above all, Mr. Hartley was a peacemaker; his self-control and his clearness of intellect made him perceive that business disasters follow quarrels. Whenever disturbed, as was rarely the case, his annoyance found expression in the low whistling of some tune; this seemed to restore his mind to its usual composure. In the many boards of directors of which he was a member, discussions of some warmth would frequently arise. On these occasions he would listen passively until he perceived that the peace of the meeting was in danger; then he would arise and, in a few well-chosen words of soothing, genial purport, turn the trend of the discussion and restore harmony. This faculty of pouring oil on troubled waters was one of his most constant traits of character in his dealings with men, and it greatly contributed to the value of his services.

Courage, as we have said, foresight and steadfastness, dominated his business career. He never embarked upon an enterprise without carefully contemplating from all points of view the chances of success. When his judgment was formed, he went to work with all his will and carried his enterprise to the end. He was never daunted by the difficulties inseparable from new undertakings, and always gave such affairs whatever attention was needful. The capital that he had collected enabled him, of course, to take advantage of situations and to push through enterprises on a large scale; but that many of these undertakings proved profitable investments is merely an instance of his courage and foresight. His reputation for sagacity naturally inspired others in any business in which he had a hand. It stood by him until the end of his life. Neither mentally nor physically did he yield to the wasting decay of age. With the advance of years, long after he had acquired a fortune with which many men of affairs would have been content to retire to relieve their minds of the burden of business and to find some rest, we see Mr. Hartley not only as vigorous and alert as in the meridian of strength and manhood, but eager to assume new responsibilities. His confidence in the future was as real as his recollection of successful deeds in the past. Yet he was as cautious as he was brave; nor would he have anything to do with any scheme unless he saw the end from the beginning. Wherein he excelled other men was the quick judgment which enabled him to decide on a course of action. Once entered upon a course, he never lost heart or faltered.

One reason for the confidence which people had in him was his reputation for honesty. In this honesty he, perhaps, displayed his greatest courage. For he was quick in the perception of right and wrong, and had the courage to be honest on all occasions. In the councils of a board of direction, in his own large business, in his intercourse with his fellow-men, and in his duties to his Creator, he could never be turned from his ideal rectitude, no matter in what position he was placed, no matter how great the temptation might be. He had a maxim in dealing with corporations which he never failed to observe—"Take care of your stockholders, and your stockholders will take care of your company." He would entertain no proposition that in the least degree tended to hurt the interests of the stockholders. His name in the directorship of a company was a guarantee for the just carrying out of its projects. Whoever wrote his name under that of Marcellus Hartley was assured of the soundness of the enterprise and of the honor and the uprightness to be observed in the administration of its affairs.

At the time of his death Mr. Hartley was but a few months less than seventy-five years of age. Fifty-eight of those years had been passed in active business, and the result for which they stand in the world of affairs was the establishing of many great and useful enterprises, the means of livelihood to hundreds of men and women, a reputation for sound judgment, integrity, and wisdom, and a name synonymous with virtue and high citizenship. To the circle of close friends they stand for a genial and vigorous personality, a quiet humor, a gentle bearing, and a sympathetic heart. To his family they mean, and will always mean, the blessed associations which cluster about the name of the considerate and dutiful son, the loyal brother, the loving husband, and the tender and righteous father. This brief memoir is but a slight sketch of the many things which serve to perpetuate the life and character of Marcellus Hartley.

# APPENDIX

# I

## PERSONAL TRIBUTES
## FROM FRIENDS OF MR. HARTLEY

*The Address of the* Right Rev. Bishop POTTER *at the
funeral services of Mr. Hartley*

IT is with exceeding regret that my friend, Dr. Parkhurst, is
obliged to absent himself on this occasion on account of illness.
I count it a privilege that, as a friend of our deceased brother,
I have been invited to take part in these services; for there is
in such an occasion as this an element of gracious symmetry,
too often, alas ! wanting when we come, amid broken hopes cut
short and lives too soon ended, to pay our tribute to one whom
God has taken to himself.

Not only in that regard had Marcellus Hartley lived out the
wonted span of life; but he had substantially lived it all here.
He was our own product;— bred and reared in this community; and doing his work, from first to last, in the eyes of
those who are represented here, and of those who have gone
before them.

There are two or three notes of such a career which we may
well recall in this place; for they were, from first to last, dis-
tinctive, and they had in Marcellus Hartley rare and inspiring
illustration.

Mr. Hartley's record in his business life was not merely able;
it was blameless.   In all his transactions the soul of honor, his
character and influence were on the side of what I may call
constructive righteousness;— that directness and integrity that
build up and conserve all honest interests upon the broad foun-
dation of honest dealing.

United with this, in a very eminent way, were insight, foresight, and grasp. We have had great merchants in New York who were no more than great shopkeepers. Mr. Hartley had, in all those relations in which he wrought and served, both vision and grasp. He saw far afield, and he seized an opportunity with that swift intuition of its values which is one of the notes, in every calling, of genius. A characteristic illustration of this was furnished during the brief and only time he held what might be called a public office. President Lincoln made him a brigadier-general of the army during the Civil War, and sent him on an important mission abroad. It was there that he listened to the speech of John Bright enlisting, in a country foreign and largely hostile to the United States, the sympathy of his hearers. Many of us would have left that hall thrilled, feeling only that we had listened to a great speaker and passed a thoroughly enjoyable night. Marcellus Hartley saw a greater opportunity in the experience. He asked permission to publish the speech and circulated it broadcast.

A wise man once defined for me the difference between the successful man and the one doomed to failure. The one is able to grasp the initiative. It was the Bright incident which showed him as the man with a genius to grasp opportunity. He possessed in the highest degree the qualities of sound judgment and exceeding coolness. I was wont to meet him when we both sought recreation from the tasks of life in the saddle, and I shall never forget the refreshment that I gained on those occasions from my intercourse with him. Each time the same kindly note rang in his voice; each time there was the same kindly smile; and I took with me from them a something indescribably comforting to my work and daily life. It was because in Marcellus Hartley was preserved that something sweet and bright with which God had blessed him at the very beginning.

Mr. Hartley's beneficence was shown in many ways besides what we know of the Hartley House. But he had a singular genius for retirement and self-effacement. Think of it! For nearly three quarters of a century he was a resident of New York and never did he hold public office! I learned only yesterday, by merest chance, that he had been a brigadier-general during the war. But to me, as to his other friends, he was never General Hartley, he was plain Marcellus Hartley. Truly, titles fall from the really great. These are some of the things for which we have to thank God this morning, the good example of His faithful servant.

I may not intrude here upon the privacy of his domestic life, nor dwell upon characteristics which revealed themselves in the more intimate relations of the home and in closer friendships. But no one could know Marcellus Hartley, even superficially, without recognizing two qualities in him, out of which come the highest types of character. He was a man of principles, and not of expediency. He was a man of heart, and not merely a man of brains. He loved his fellow-men and gladly served them, and in all the relations of life he brought to them that singular charm of gracious courtesy, of inextinguishable cheerfulness, of sunny sweetness of behavior and of presence, which makes us feel to-day that here a light has gone out. Thank God, we know, as he knew, that in God's plan it was not to be quenched, and will not be; but only transplanted to shine with undimmed luster in the perfect presence and by the perfect light.

*An Article by the* Rev. Dr. PARKHURST, *in the "Christian Work," entitled*

## MARCELLUS HARTLEY

I HAVE not put this name at the head of my article for any purpose of eulogy. A man who did not care to be complimented while he was living would resent having advantage taken of his absence to compliment him after he is dead.

Nor need it be said that the reference here made to Mr. Hartley is not because of the large wealth of which he stood possessed prior to his decease. No one will be disposed to deny, presumably, that when men as wealthy as he die, there is a natural and a carnal impulse to make much of the occasion simply out of regard to the immensity of the dead man's pecuniary accumulations. All such impulse, however, is distinctly pagan, and can have no legitimate place in the consciousness of a Christian or in the means employed for the celebration or perpetuation of his memory.

Speaking of eulogies, it needs to be said that one reason why we are often constrained to speak pleasantly of the dead is that we suddenly realize that we only imperfectly appreciated them while they were still living, and would like to make good previous omission; and it is certainly true that our consciousness of estimable traits rarely becomes adequate and complete till the man or woman in whom they inhere is gone. It is regrettable that our admirations are so sadly belated. Mr. Depew stated this in his after-dinner style when he said that he preferred taffy to epitaph-y. When we read at Woodlawn the inscriptions on the tombs of the dead and remember that those living down in the city will have much the same inscriptions put on their monuments by and by—and very likely deservedly—it sets us reflecting on the excellence of the people we are living among, and encourages in us the spirit of ante-mortem appreciation.

There is, then, one feature in Mr. Hartley's character that I should like to specify, not at all in any spirit of compliment to him or his memory, but because it is something to be thought about by those of us who believe theoretically in the truth and in telling the truth, but who, as matter of practice, are willing on occasion to depart from the truth far enough to serve present interest and convenience. I doubt if Mr. Hartley was morally capable of telling a lie, or of consciously accommodating the truth to a momentary exigency. It is often remarked that business men have one reputation downtown and another reputation uptown, but it is in view of what I know of his downtown reputation that I am emboldened to say that in his judgment there was no neutral territory between a truth and a lie, and that the instant truth stops lie begins, and that he never consciously stepped across the line.

There was very little dogma in Mr. Hartley's religion, and very little emotion, but the line of rectitude meant the same thing to him that the plumb-line does to the mason, and he built to it. And that was one ingredient in what was known as his financial farsightedness. He may or may not have had a keener eye than many others, but at any rate there was no dust in his eye. Consequently many questions that were problems to others were no problems to him, but axioms. The inner truthfulness of the man rendered distinct the outlines of the matters he had to deal with, and so made conclusions easy.

He was, therefore, a man to tie to. He was one of those fixed centers around which the machinery of the financial world was able to turn without racking itself in the revolution. Such men are what make a business world possible. Wall Street can exist not because there are so many liars and thieves in it, but because there are so many, like Mr. Hartley, who recognize the fact that community of interest and of relations is made possible by the number of people that believe in truth and that stand by their word. Clergymen who avail of Wall Street to point their homilies on fraud do so because they don't know or because they want to be smart.

It would be difficult to conceive of a volume more interesting and illuminating than the one Mr. Hartley might have written portraying, from his standpoint as Christian and successful man of affairs, his knowledge of men and things gained by a half century of intimate experience.

A sample of what such a volume might have contained is afforded by a single remark that he dropped in course of a conversation I had with him at his house some time ago. I had recently said something in a public way bearing upon the character and performances of a man of our State whose business connections are in this city, though not himself a citizen here. Mr. Hartley asked me abruptly, "What is the particular thing that Mr. —— is doing that in your judgment warrants your regarding him with so much suspicion and disfavor?" My answer was, "You are aware, Mr. Hartley, that we have recently been proving to the satisfaction of the public that there is in this city a compact between the criminal classes and the official classes, by virtue of which criminals have certain immunities allowed them in return for the money they pay over to the police, and that the wardman is the intermediary between the contracting parties. Now, my conception of Mr. —— is that he is a sort of wardman, the go-between between the corporations and the Legislature, and he handles the 'stuff' which the corporations put up, the payment of which secures them legislative favor." Mr. Hartley was always laconic in his style, and the only reply he made was, "That is about the size of it; I have had opportunity to know." I refer to this only as an illustration of the flood of light that in so many ways could be thrown upon both the bright and the dark side of our city by one so long and so intimately at home as Mr. Hartley with what goes to make up the city's life.

The stamp which by his career of uncompromising integrity he has, for so long a term of years, been putting upon the business character of our town is one not easy to be effaced. We wish that his career of example and precept might have been longer continued. We wish that he had consented to allow to exhausted body and wearied mind that occasional term of relaxation which such a life of mental strain demands; but it is for each man to judge for himself how he can best fulfil his mission. Certain it is that from a life of such prolonged toil and incessant responsibility no exit could have been more congenial to him than that which fell to his lot, to arrive at the end with native force unabated, and to fall with his armor on, in the midst of the congenial and sympathetic spirits that had been so long his comrades in the battle.

## *A Letter from* Mr. ANDREW CARNEGIE

THE first thought of my friend Marcellus Hartley always crystallizes with the word *Character,*— a man of principle, straight as an arrow, his word as good as his bond.

Then comes to me his loyalty to his selected friends. He did not choose friends hastily, could not have had many in the core of his heart; he was much too positive and clear in his likings and judgment to be hail-fellow with the multitude.

Those to whom he felt drawn must have at base similar virtues to his own. This is always the case with strong personalities. Many liked and all respected him, and many he liked but only the special few who were true he hooked to himself with bands of steel. Younger than himself, I had reason to note and appreciate this lovable trait. The days he called were red-letter days to me, and a growing appreciation of the man was one of my pleasures. I felt more and more drawn to him, until at last he became one to whom I felt, if I needed counsel, yes, or assistance, I should go at once, well assured I should not go in vain. He was a tower of strength to friends in trouble. In the whole range of my acquaintance I know of no one who personified more fully all the virtues of the men of affairs. He was the Captain of Industry in whom deceit, misrepresentation, and sharp practice found no resting-place, a man with whom one could shake hands and rest certain that to the end he had a colleague who, come what might, would be found laboring side by side in perfect good faith. He never deserted an individual or a cause he had once espoused.

Mr. Hartley had some conversations with me upon the final disposition of his great fortune, and was to take up that subject with me upon our return to New York in the autumn. He was deeply concerned, and resolved to place his affairs in order without delay, and he had lofty plans in view. Alas! the summons came before we could meet again, and friendly conferences were at an end.

He has passed from among us, but the memory of a true man and loyal friend remains to us who knew him well; nor will the day come, while memory remains, when I can forget Marcellus Hartley.

SKIBO CASTLE, August, 1902.

## *A Letter from* Mr. WILLIAM A. WHEELOCK

MARCELLUS HARTLEY was one of my dearest friends for many years, and the removal by death of no one outside of my own family could have come nearer to me. The confidence between us was mutual and close, and the almost daily relations between us in the several institutions in which we were associated cemented a friendship to be broken only by death. The fact that at one of these frequent meetings the silent message came to him, while his hand was in my own, I can never forget. The scene is constantly before me. I miss his companionship every day.

In estimating the character and life of Mr. Hartley, there are two distinct sides. In the business world, where his success was phenomenal and complete, everything was compelled to bow to the mandate of his judgment, which seemed unerring, and the results achieved in his lifelong career fully justified the soundness of his judgment. No one could question his preëminence as one of the master minds in the commercial world.

To me, however, the great charm of Mr. Hartley's character lay in his unaffected simplicity, his noble Christian life, and the intense loyalty to the memory of his distinguished father which he cherished. He was proud of his father's active interest in every worthy charity; and in the many confidential talks we had as to the responsibilities of successful men, he seemed anxious and determined that his own name and memory should be equally identified in the future with large and worthy charities.

There were no striking incidents connected with my association with Mr. Hartley; many of those in his earlier life have been so well portrayed by himself that they have become almost historic, and the records of our Civil War would not be complete without them.

This is but a mere tribute to the life and character of my dear Mr. Hartley, whose many virtues I shall ever remember.

## *A Tribute from* Mr. JAMES W. ALEXANDER

MARCELLUS HARTLEY was one of the most remarkable men I have ever met. I had some opportunity to know, for he was in and out of my office almost every day during the last ten years of his life. He served on the Executive Committee of the Equitable Society, which held three sessions a week, and he generally dropped in on other days, also. Mr. Hartley constantly reminded me of the proverb, "Seest thou a man diligent in his business? He shall stand before kings; he shall not stand before mean men." He was the most industrious man I ever knew. He began in that way and kept it up until the minute he died, at the age of seventy-four. He often told me that he got his amusement out of his business. He rode horseback every afternoon, but he did it systematically to keep his health robust. He took little part in society affairs, but was generally at home in the evening, where he read a great deal. He had the habit of disposing at once of anything he had to do, and put in his work steadily throughout the day.

He directed enormous concerns of his own. The Union Metallic Cartridge Company, which he practically owned, is, I suppose, the largest thing of its kind in the world, and this was only one of a number of such commercial and manufacturing enterprises which he managed. He supplied arms to all nations. He kept his eye on everything and never took his finger off the lever. Even when he went on a vacation he kept up constant communication. Notwithstanding his own vast interests, he entered intelligently and diligently into the affairs of the companies of which he was a director. He was not a perfunctory director; he informed himself and he worked.

In our own company he was a useful and wise coadjutor. It amazed me to see how interested he would become in matters outside the sphere in which he made his money. At the very time of his death he was occupying his mind, time, and talents in developing a new financial organization of world-wide importance, and had been in my office talking with me about it in the most enthusiastic strain fifteen minutes before he died. He had strong likes and dislikes, but they were always based on reasons—not mere prejudice. When he liked a man he stood by him through thick and thin. He was ready to back up his opinions and his friendships with his credit and his money.

He was a very shrewd business man, with great courage when he had made up his mind. He was not a speculator. He was one of the earliest to see the practical future of electricity and invested in it.

When he began his business career he introduced new and resolute methods. He told me once that he had secured all the mosaics in Florence that could be bought, and all the red coral in Naples, to the astonishment of the dealers, and made much money by bringing them to this country for sale. This was when his business was in various kinds of merchandise. Afterward he became a great manufacturer. He knew and was known by every important man in New York, but he never sought prominence. He was gentle and companionable, but stern and unyielding when he thought principles were involved.

A book embodying nothing but his own experiences would make a thrilling volume. During the Civil War he visited Europe and bought arms for our government, and thwarted the efforts of the South in the same direction.

Time will not suffice to give even a sketch of his career and character. But he was a marked man. His relations to charities and works of beneficence form another side which it is hoped may yet be made public. He had no counterpart that I know of. He was original and he was eminent in his domain. His loss will be keenly felt. But he died as he lived — in the harness.

## A Letter from Mr. George Gould

I HAVE known him for twenty years, and he has always been one of my closest friends and associates. I met him to-day at a Director's meeting and was deeply grieved at the news of his sudden death. He had a charming personality and was a good business man with excellent judgment. He had hosts of friends, who appreciate his kindly ways, and who, I am sure, will be deeply grieved at his death.

## A Letter from Mr. James H. Hyde

MR. HARTLEY became a Director of the Equitable Life Assurance Society of the United States (founded by my father, Henry B. Hyde, in 1859) at the close of the year 1884. I was elected a member of that Board in 1895, and was closely associated with Mr. Hartley until the day of his death; indeed, he attended a meeting of the Executive Committee of the Equitable Society on the day of his death. He was a zealous member of that Committee, whose chief province it is to find investment for the assets of the Society, and he saw these assets grow from fifty-eight millions in 1884, when he became a member of our Board, to more than three hundred and thirty millions at the time of his death.

A minute account of Mr. Hartley's career would furnish an adequate history of the development of American manufacture and finance during the generation to which he belonged. The scope of his experience, the number of great enterprises with which he was identified directly or indirectly, his intimacy with the prominent men of his time, made his reminiscences exceedingly interesting; and when among his intimate friends, after telling some interesting experience in connection with the Civil War, or the laying of the Atlantic cable, or political conflicts, or labor disturbances, or financial panics, he was often urged in my hearing to put his reminiscences in writing for permanent preservation.

Mr. Hartley was a man so quiet and unobtrusive that the casual observer little suspected his strength of character, but he was a man of strong individuality, keen intellect, and inquisitive eagerness to get to the bottom of things. Perhaps his chief characteristic was his tenacity of purpose, the courage with which, after satisfying himself with the soundness of an enterprise, he backed it up until success had been attained. Most of the enterprises in which he was directly interested succeeded because he was never afraid to send what seemed to be good money after bad in order to make what appeared to be a forlorn hope a brilliant triumph.

Mr. Hartley and my father were among the first men in this country to invest their money in electricity, and for a number of years there were periods when spectators prophesied nothing but disaster; but Mr. Hartley never faltered, and every one knows the result. Mr. Hartley and my father were close friends and intimately associated in business for nearly a quarter of a century. Mr. Hartley outlived my father scarcely more than two and a half years.

## *A Letter from* Mr. D. Willis James

Mr. Marcellus Hartley was so long a prominent figure among the successful merchants of New York that his removal leaves a large vacant place. His life is an object-lesson to young men. Starting at the bottom, he quickly won a commanding position, and during our Civil War, forty years ago, he was a conspicuous figure and had large and very important trusts thrust upon him. He always proved himself to be fully equal to meet all demands made upon him.

He was long recognized as one of the ablest and most successful manufacturers in the country. As a financier he held a high position, and as a negotiator he had few, if any, equals.

Mr. Hartley was modest and unassuming; one had to know him well fully to recognize his abilities and the breadth of his view.

He was a man to be trusted and to be depended upon in all the relations of life. He was not carried off his balance by prosperity, and was always calm in every storm.

He continued to the last a regular attendant on the church of his fathers and a supporter of the institutions of religion.

His removal is greatly deplored by a large number of devoted friends.

## *A Tribute from* Hon. Chauncey M. Depew

The first I heard of the death of Marcellus Hartley was when the pilot brought the newspapers aboard. Mr. Hartley and I were close friends for over forty years, and he was a lovable, splendid man. He was one of our very big men of affairs. His judgment in business was absolutely unerring. If he had written his autobiography, it would have proven a marvelously interesting book. With his unerring business judgment and great foresight, he amassed a great fortune.

When the amount of his estate is known, it will be a vast surprise to those who did not really know the quiet man of affairs.

Few of our citizens have done greater service to the United States. In civil life, he was a great factor in the strife of the States. His services to the Union were of the utmost importance. He not only succeeded in controlling the arms for the Northern armies, but he kept the Confederacy from obtaining arms. We did not then understand gun-making, and by visits to the factories he learned the secrets of gun-metals and mechanism, which were invaluable to the Federal Government. A very great man, a true friend and real patriot, has gone.

## *A Letter from* Mr. John Crosby Brown

My most vivid recollections of Mr. Hartley are connected with his life on Orange Mountain. In the earlier years of our residence there it was Mr. Hartley's habit, on summer evenings after the close of a busy day in New York, to spend part of the evening on the piazza of Dr. William Adams's house, in company with General George B. McClellan and General Randolph B. Marcy, when the conversation turned on various incidents of the Civil War in which they each took so prominent a part. Dr. Adams had the faculty of bringing out on such occasions special points in which the various persons present had been actively engaged, and members of our different families would gather to hear the story of some incident on a famous battle-field, or a visit to the Army of the Potomac in connection with the Christian Commission. At times General Marcy would relate his early experiences on the frontier, fascinating his hearers by many a thrilling incident of Indian adventure; and then, after Mr. Hartley had been a silent listener, Dr. Adams would turn to him, and in his persuasive way draw out the story of his life and work in England as the representative of the United States Government in the purchase of arms and ammunition for the Federal army. His modesty in minimizing the valuable service that he rendered at that time made a great impression upon those who were his listeners.

A marked trait in his character that impressed me at all times was his courtesy to elderly people. I have before me the very vivid picture of his kindness and courtesy to my father and mother in their old age, notably at Saratoga, on the piazza of the old United States Hotel, when he never failed to do all in his power to make the afternoons and evenings pleasant for his old friends.

I can say little about his business career; for, while I saw much of him in our country home and in New York in the winter, we had very few business transactions together, and in our busy lives we seldom met downtown.

## *A Letter from* Mr. ANSON PHELPS STOKES

I KNEW Marcellus Hartley for about thirty-five years. His father I also well remember when I was a boy; he and my father were associated in charitable work for improving the condition of the poor.

The first conversation with Marcellus Hartley that I recall was, I think, about 1864, when, for the Ansonia Brass and Copper Company, I made with him an important contract for cartridge metal, and I made similar contracts with him in succeeding years. In our discussion regarding these contracts, I was impressed with his business ability and foresight, and I was well satisfied with the manner in which he carried out his agreements regardless of the course of the market. I became convinced that he was, or would soon be, the leading man in the ammunition business of the country.

When I was in the banking business in Wall Street, he came to see me, and invited me to become interested with him in a company for the development of electric lighting, regarding which he had been experimenting at Bridgeport. I became a director with him in this company, which he, with a few friends, controlled. I had a good opportunity to confirm my opinion as to his very great ability and high business character.

I have seen him sitting almost silent during a discussion at a board meeting, and then ask some important question, or express in few words some judgment, which, in the decision of the matters before us, had more influence than all that had been said by the other members.

As a business adviser in important matters I think he was recognized in a number of boards as the wisest head, and he commonly did much more than his share of the work.

He had a pleasant and cheerful manner which made people like to see him, and which, with the knowledge that he would stand by what he said, greatly facilitated the carrying out of important affairs.

It was also pleasant to note, as I had repeated occasion to do, that, notwithstanding the excessive business cares which oppressed him, he was glad to give attention to charitable work at Hartley House and elsewhere.

Our intercourse through these many years led me to esteem him highly. What Bishop Potter said at the funeral contained much that I, in common with other friends, have felt, but could not so well express.

### *A Letter from* Mr. GEORGE WESTINGHOUSE

IT affords me much pleasure to say that my associations with Mr. Marcellus Hartley gave me an opportunity to become well acquainted with him and to appreciate his many most excellent qualities. I regarded his judgment in many matters in which we were mutually interested as of the highest importance, and it was always to my regret that we had not become acquainted at a much earlier period and at a time when coöperation between us might have led to greater results in the development of the electrical enterprise in which we both took so much interest.

He was always cordial and consistent, and always ready to render valuable assistance. His death caused me much sorrow, because it brought to an end relations which had grown to be pleasant in every way.

### *A Letter from* Hon. LEVI P. MORTON

I AM pleased to know that a memoir of Marcellus Hartley is being prepared. It is only proper that some permanent memorial, which will in some degree do justice to his character and his services to the community, should be put in a form which will be acceptable to his many friends. I had the pleasure of knowing him for many years in business and social relations, and always held the highest opinion of his business abilities, integrity, and kindly nature. The community suffered a severe loss in his death.

### *A Letter from* Rev. ROBERT S. McGREGOR

MY acquaintance with Marcellus Hartley extended over a period of three years. From formality it merged into informality, and so into friendship. I knew him best in his St. Cloud home, where for two weeks I stayed as his guest. Shall I ever forget them,—those evenings spent in front of the blazing hearth; the insight he gave me into his early life, the stories he told me of the war, of Lincoln, of Grant, of those awful nights in Birmingham, England, and in Paris! Or, again, shall I ever forget the stories of his struggles in the business world, or his association with men socially and politically, many of whom gave worth and character to our country's progress!

But all these stories would have lost value to the writer did not their narration possess one quality — modesty. To the slavery question there was to him only one side — the Northern. He believed with his friend, Mr. Lincoln, that all men are created free and equal, and to this end he ever worked. He was a Republican in politics, but democratic in heart, not easily appealed to, but once interested in a cause he remained firm to the end.

Of his business life I need say little. There are those who knew him in this capacity better than I; but of him an old business friend said to me: "Mr. Hartley was a shrewd, but an honest business man; you knew where to find him, and so knew how to approach him."

Mr. Hartley allowed no dictation; his conscience governed his thought and actions. Questions of church, of charities private and public, as well as questions of business, appealed to him only as they appealed through his conscience. Sentiment and public notoriety played no part. He gave of his purse and of his time in the most unostentatious way. In so doing, he filled a place in the hearts and lives of many men, who to-day mourn his loss, but who cherish, and ever will cherish, his memory.

*A Poem by* Miss ALINE CHESTER WHITE, *in the*
"*New York Observer*"

A CALM and holy light is breaking
   Through the darkened sunset sky,
And a life now fully ended
   Has ascended upon high.

His was one of noble action
   In the noonday and the heat,
Filled he all of life's great duties,
   Leaves it perfect, all complete.

Filled with modest grace and sweetness,
   Without trouble, toil, or pain,
Soared his soul to worlds unknown,
   And our loss becomes his gain.

See, his light is gently shedding
   Radiant beams upon each one,
And to us the words are borne,
   That his work has been " well done."

Lo ! his life work now all ended,
   Ready for his great reward ;
With a smile upon his lips
   His soul ascended to its Lord.

# II

## RESOLUTIONS AND
## MINUTES OF CORPORATIONS WITH WHICH
## MR. HARTLEY WAS CONNECTED

### *The Association for Improving the*
### *Condition of the Poor*

#### MINUTE

IN entering upon their records mention of the death of the late Marcellus Hartley, the Board of Managers cannot but recall that he came fairly by the qualities which made his name everywhere respected. His father, the first secretary of this Association and to all intents and purposes its founder, illustrated all through his official life the same qualities which, later on, gave the younger Hartley his good name. Keenness of insight, thoroughness of method, absolute integrity of purpose, were characteristic of both of them; and although in lives of father and son, the respective fields upon which these characteristics were illustrated were widely different, we may trace the successful careers of both men to one and the same source.

To the memory of Robert Milham Hartley, the naming of Hartley House was a deserved tribute, while for the maintenance of the activities of that institution and the extending of its borders, we are largely indebted to the wise generosity and timely counsel of our late associate.

At a critical period in the history of the nation, Marcellus Hartley rendered his country a service which can never be forgotten; but it may be questioned whether from that achievement he himself drew any deeper satisfaction than came to him in his latest years from watching over and fostering the work founded in his father's name. Alike as a patriot and as a practical philanthropist, he has left a record of which those who were honored by his friendship may be justly proud.

I hereby certify that the above is a true copy of the minute adopted by the Board of Managers at the regular meeting held February 17th, 1902.

L. E. OPDYCKE,
*Secretary.*

## *The Westinghouse Electric and Manufacturing Company*

*Whereas*, Marcellus Hartley, a member of the Board of Direction of this Company for more than ten years, died on January 8th, 1902, therefore

*Resolved:* The Board of Directors desires to bear testimony to the value of Mr. Hartley as a brother director. The long term of Mr. Hartley's service included the period during which a re-organization of the Company had to be effected, under circumstances of great financial difficulty, with impaired resources, and in the midst of a well nigh unprecedented business depression.

Throughout that trying experience there was no person connected with the Company in any capacity of greater service to it than Mr. Hartley. His courage ever rose to the occasion; and it was always during periods of greatest stress that his presence in the Board was most indispensable. From first to last, by his business experience and sagacity, his sound judgment and large resources, he contributed potently to the preservation and development of the property and the protection and profit of its stock-holders. The loss this Board and the Company have sustained through his death is one which it can hardly be hoped will be made good.

The other directors deem it proper formally to record this evidence of the estimation in which Mr. Hartley was held by them, of the service he rendered, and of their sense of the loss incurred through his death.

*Resolved*, That this vote be entered in full on the records of the Board, and the Secretary be instructed to send an engrossed copy thereof to the family of Mr. Hartley, indicative of the sympathy felt in their loss by his business associates.

At a meeting of the Board of Directors of the Westinghouse Electric and Manufacturing Company held at New York, January 23rd, 1902, the foregoing resolutions were unanimously adopted.

GEORGE WESTINGHOUSE,
*President.*

BRAYTON IVES,
*Chairman.*

CHARLES FRANCIS ADAMS
AUGUST BELMONT
ANTHONY N. BRADY
N. WILLIS BUMSTED
GEORGE W. HEBARD
JAMES H. HYDE
FRANK H. TAYLOR
GEORGE C. SMITH
B. H. WARREN
H. H. WESTINGHOUSE
*Directors.*

CHARLES A. TERRY,
*Secretary.*

## *The Manhattan Railway Company*

AT a meeting of the Directors of the Manhattan Railway Company, held on Tuesday, a copy of the following resolutions was ordered to be sent to the family of the late Marcellus Hartley:

MARCELLUS HARTLEY has gone to his well-earned rest. He died in the full enjoyment of life, in the midst of his activities, with usefulness unimpaired. The light of his intelligence did not fade slowly and flickeringly, but was suddenly quenched, with its brightness undiminished.

Apart from the shock to friends and to those who stood closest to him, thus suddenly and dreadfully bereaved, it is a happy ending that leaves no memory behind but that of complete and unimpaired intellectual power.

The life thus rudely ended was one that had been freely used in the service of others, and, for that reason, productive of happiness to its possessor. Gifted by nature with energy, discernment, industry, and integrity, possessed of a moral nature that kept his high order of intelligence always on the side of the right, Marcellus Hartley was necessarily a successful man in his business life, and largely benefited by the exercise of his talents. He was not content, however, with using his great abilities and the material resources they brought him, merely in the service of himself and those immediately dependent upon him.

While yet a comparatively young man, the needs of his country during the Civil War called for the successful use of his abilities in foreign service of a delicate and highly important character.

During his entire life as Director in corporations, as adviser of those who sought his counsel, his time, his energies, and his thoughts were freely given in the service of others and in directions where his private interests were small indeed compared to his gifts of time and careful thought.

His private as well as his public charities stamped him as one who loved his fellow-man, and who realized that the road to personal happiness was most surely trodden by him whose thoughts were given to smoothing for others the ruggedness of life's paths. His cheerfulness and buoyancy of disposition enlivened the dry details of business life, and his wise and penetrating intelligence never failed to further discussion in the direction of safe conclusion.

The Directors of the Manhattan Railway Company realize that they have lost a valued associate, a sagacious counsellor, and a personal friend, and hereby make record of their sense of loss and of their deep sympathy with the bereaved ones from whom Marcellus Hartley has been thus suddenly taken away.

## *The American Surety Company of New York*

AT a regular quarterly meeting of the Board of Trustees of the American Surety Company of New York, held Wednesday, January 15, 1902, the following minute was presented by Mr. William A. Wheelock, and unanimously adopted:

IN the sudden death of Mr. Marcellus Hartley, not only the American Surety Company, of whose Executive Committee he was an active member, but every institution in our city with whose interests he was identified have experienced a loss which cannot be estimated.

Failure with him in any department of business life, was never to be predicated of anything to which he gave his confidence, his time, and his personality.

The history of our city, for the last fifty years of its active and marvellous improvements, would not be complete without at least a partial record of his active career, and no one can ever know how many thriving and now prosperous industries are indebted to his bold and courageous help, in the time of almost despair, when, in his masterful way, he spoke the word which brought relief, and assured success.

Unassuming always, he rather shrank from than courted prominence, and in all the daily cares of his busy life he passed in and out before his associates in his tireless round of duty, ever calm and deliberate, until, touched by the hand of death in our very presence, he passed in a moment from our sight, consecrating, as it were, the spot in which, as associates, we had so often met.

His life is one long eulogy, and we enter this minute upon our records, conveying to the family of our deceased friend, our most sincere condolence in this hour of their bereavement.

DAVID B. SICKELS,
*Vice-President.*

## The Western National Bank

AT a regular meeting of the Board of Directors of the Western National Bank, held on Wednesday, the fifteenth of January, Nineteen hundred and two, the following preamble and resolution was unanimously adopted:

*Whereas*, the sudden death of our associate, Marcellus Hartley, on the eighth day of January entails a loss to this bank which it would be difficult to measure.

For many years past Mr. Hartley has been an active director, and more recently one of the Vice-Presidents of the

Bank. As was his habit in regard to all enterprises with which he was connected, he kept himself constantly informed of the operations of the institution, and lent to it his valuable experience, industry, and financial skill. He took an earnest part in the proceedings of the Executive Committee, and was ever ready to lend the weight of his character, credit, means, and talents to the building up of an enterprise which has now assumed proportions and reached a firm condition recognized by all observers.

*Resolved,* That the Board of Directors of the Western National Bank do hereby record their profound grief at the removal of so useful and devoted a friend.

*Resolved,* That the minute be entered on the records of the Bank as a sincere, though inadequate, expression of the sentiments of this Board, and that a copy of the same be sent to the family of the deceased.

### *The Mercantile Trust Company*

AT a meeting of the Board of Directors of the Mercantile Trust Company, held on Wednesday, January 15th, 1902, the following resolution was adopted:

*Resolved,* That the death of Mr. Marcellus Hartley has brought to the members of this Board a deep sorrow for the loss of one whom all had learned to honor and cherish.

Mr. Hartley first became a Director of the Company in December, 1881, and from that time has always been one of its ablest advisers and strongest supporters.

Mr. Hartley was elected a member of the Examining Committee in November, 1881, and of the Executive Committee of the Board of Directors in September, 1884, and has since been most earnest in his zeal for the growth and prosperity of the Company.

We deeply mourn our loss and sincerely sympathize with the family in their affliction.

ERNEST R. ADEE,
*Secretary.*

## *The International Banking Corporation*

AT a meeting of the Board of Directors of the International Banking Corporation, held in the City of New York on Wednesday, January twenty-second, Nineteen Hundred and two, the following resolution was unanimously adopted and an engrossed copy ordered to be sent to Mr. Hartley's family.

AN all wise Providence having taken from this life our honored and esteemed friend, the President of this Corporation, Mr. Marcellus Hartley, we take this occasion to convey to his bereaved family our heartfelt sympathy.

We are grateful that we were permitted to know him and to work with him.

Having long since chosen the Christian life as the ideal one, he gave himself heartily to all forms of activity and loved especially to be identified with undertakings that would be of benefit to this community and to his loved country.

In the midst of his work, while "his eye was not dim, nor his natural force abated" and in the act of speaking kindly words, his final summons came.

His was an ideal life and in many respects an ideal death.

| | |
|---|---|
| THOMAS H. HUBBARD, | EUGENE DELANO, |
| JAMES W. ALEXANDER, | J. M. CEBALLOS, |
| ABRAM S. HEWITT, | H. E. MANNING, |
| V. P. SNYDER, | EDWARD F. CRAGIN. |

JOHN I. McCOOK.

## *The Lincoln National Bank of the City of New York*

NEW YORK, January 16th, 1902.

THE Board of Directors has learned with feelings of deep regret of the sudden death of Marcellus Hartley, for eleven years a director of this Institution.

The Board desires to place upon record its appreciation of the high character, great ability, and sterling integrity of the deceased and to extend to his bereaved family its deepest sympathy at this time of their great affliction.

*Resolved*, That a copy of this minute, properly engrossed, be sent to the family of the deceased.

THOMAS L. JAMES,
*President.*

WILLIAM T. CORNELL,
*Cashier.*

## *The Fifth Avenue Trust Company*

AT a meeting of the Board of Trustees of the Fifth Avenue Trust Company, held on February eleventh, Nineteen hundred and Two, the following minute was unanimously adopted:

MR. GERRY offered the following as a minute to be spread upon the record of the Company.

This Board has learned with great sorrow of the sudden death of its valued member, Marcellus Hartley, who, as one of the founders of the Company, and from its inception a member of the Executive Committee, has freely given his time and counsel to our interests. We record here our appreciation of his service. His long and useful career in mercantile and financial affairs in this city, his knowledge of credits and values, his zeal in the interests of every corporation to which he lent his name, his singular punctuality and attention in the performance of his duties, and his uniform modesty and courtesy form the framework of his outward life, while his strength of character, his unswerving integrity in purpose and action, his patriotic feeling, his devotion to good works for mankind, and his sense of duty to every trust committed to his care, portray the friend and associate whose memory we cherish and whose loss we mourn.

## *The American Deposit and Loan Company*

AT a regular meeting of the Board of Trustees of the American Deposit and Loan Company, held on Tuesday, January fourteenth, Nineteen Hundred and Two, the following resolution was unanimously adopted:

*Resolved*, That this Board desires to record the great loss which it has sustained in the death of its late member, Marcellus Hartley.

He was highly esteemed by his business associates for his wide and accurate information, his prudence, sound judgment, great integrity, and genial character.

This Board, in particular, will miss his wise advice and devotion to its interests.

BOARD OF TRUSTEES.

| | |
|---|---|
| JAMES H. HYDE, | GEORGE W. JENKINS, |
| EDWARD H. HARRIMAN, | OTTO H. KAHN, |
| G. E. TARBELL, | J. HENRY SMITH, |
| GEORGE H. SQUIRE, | CHARLES B. ALEXANDER, |
| H. M. ALEXANDER, | BAINBRIDGE COLBY, |
| WM. H. MCINTYRE, | HENRY ROGERS WINTHROP, |
| V. P. SNYDER, | BRADISH JOHNSON, |
| THOMAS H. HUBBARD, | LOUIS FITZGERALD, |

WILLIAM ALEXANDER.

## *The German American Bank*

AT a meeting of the German American Bank, held on January fourteenth, Nineteen Hundred and Two, the following resolutions were unanimously adopted.

*Whereas*, It has pleased Providence to remove from our midst and from his sphere of usefulness Marcellus Hartley, our late associate in this Board, therefore —

*Resolved*, That in the death of Mr. Hartley this Board mourns the loss of one whose character and ability always commanded our highest admiration and confidence.

*Resolved*, That we tender to his widow and family our heartfelt sympathies for this great affliction they have been called upon to sustain.

*Resolved*, That a copy of these resolutions be forwarded to the family of the deceased and be entered upon our minutes.

CASIMIR TAG,
*President.*

J. F. FREDERICHS,
*Cashier.*

## *The Audit Company of New York*

AT a special meeting of the Audit Company of New York, held to-day, the following resolutions were adopted.

*Whereas*, The death of Marcellus Hartley has deprived this Company of a valued and esteemed Director: be it

*Resolved*, That we sincerely lament the loss which has befallen the community from the death of a most useful citizen, whose many years were full of examples of untiring endeavor, earnest patriotism, broad charity, and kindly personal consideration of all with whom he was associated; and be it further

*Resolved*, That a copy of this resolution, with the signatures attached thereto, be sent to the bereaved family.

| | |
|---|---|
| AUGUST BELMONT, | A. J. CASSATT, |
| JOSEPH S. AUERBACH. | W. A. NASH, |
| JOHN I. WATERBURY, | JAMES STILLMAN, |
| CHARLES R. FLINT, | G. G. HAVEN, |
| GEORGE HARVEY, | G. W. YOUNG. |

NEW YORK, January 10, 1902.

## *The Remington Arms Company*

AT a meeting of the employees of the Remington Arms Company, held in the Village Hall, Friday evening, January 10th, 1902, the following resolutions were adopted:

*Whereas*, the employees of the Remington Arms Company learn with regret of the sudden death of Marcellus Hartley, the esteemed president of this Company and,

*Whereas*, the loss sustained by the commercial world in general and particularly by the corporations with which he has been closely connected will be deeply felt and his place among the great financiers of the country will be filled with difficulty,—

*Resolved*, That we tender our sincere and heartfelt sympathy to the members of Mr. Hartley's family in their deep bereavement.

JAMES A. WHITFIELD,
L. N. WALKER,
ALONZO A. RIVERS,
*Committee.*

ILION, NEW YORK, January 10th, 1902.

## *The Gun and Sporting Goods Trade*

AT a special meeting of the Gun and Sporting Goods Trade, held January tenth, Nineteen Hundred and Two, the following minute was adopted.

IN obedience to the omnipotent decree, in a moment as in the "twinkling of an eye," Marcellus Hartley has been called from us.

His name has been associated with all our business undertakings.

For many years he has stood forth clearly as the leading figure in the trade to which nearly all his life was devoted, and from which the many various enterprises that sought his counsel in later years were not able to weaken his allegiance.

His indomitable will, ceaseless energy, and untiring perseverance make a standard to which few can attain.

His integrity of character, faithfulness of purpose, largeness of view, and keenness of discernment made him more and more sought as a leader and advisor.

Until the last moment of his life he was a man of affairs.

In recognition of his worth we desire to record this tribute of honor, regard, and esteem.

U. T. HUNGERFORD,
*Chairman.*

JOSEPH GALES,
*Secretary.*

U. T. HUNGERFORD BRASS & COPPER CO.,

U. T. HUNGERFORD,
*President.*

WINCHESTER REPEATING ARMS CO.,

T. G. BENNETT,
*President.*

G. E. HODSON,
*Vice-president.*

A. G. Spalding & Bros.,    J. W. Curtiss,
*Secretary.*

The H. & D. Folsom }    Henry T. Folsom,
     Arms Co.,      }            *President.*

Von Lengerke & Detmold,
A. H. Funke,
J. H. Lau & Co.,
M. W. Robinson Co.,    R. M. Nesbith,
                              *President.*

Charles J. Godfrey,
The Iver-Johnson Arms & Cycle Works,
Tower & Lyon,
William M. Odell,
George G. Moore,
William P. Howell,
H. H. Kiffe,
William M. Cornwall,
Jespersen & Hines,
H. Werlemann,
Schoverling, Daly & Gales.    Charles Howard Daly,
                                   *Secretary.*

# III

## EDITORIAL COMMENT ON MR. HARTLEY'S DEATH

### *From the "New York Times"*

#### MARCELLUS HARTLEY

STRICKEN at the council-table in the performance of deliberative and advisory duties for which his long experience and remarkable powers of sound judgment gave him so high a degree of fitness, Marcellus Hartley may be said to have died as the wise man might wish to die: not after a period of pain and in weakness, but with the harness on, in the fullness of his powers, and in attendance upon his daily tasks. For the friends of Mr. Hartley there is also consoling force in the reflection that, measured either by achievements, or by the reputation, the distinction, and the public and private esteem he had won, his life was an unusually full one.

No man in the history of affairs in this city of Mr. Hartley's wide range of activities, real power, and recognized influence was ever more modest and unassuming. Quite unknown to the multitudes who saw him every day, and by strong personal disinclination a stranger to the arts by which public fame is acquired, Mr. Hartley was, and for more than a quarter of a century has been, one of the strong and influential figures in the financial circles of New York. His judgment was valued and his advice sought by men who are themselves of commanding importance. He was, indeed, one of the surest and wisest counselors in all commercial and investment undertakings. Forty years ago, when Mr. Hartley was a young man, the United States Government intrusted to him the performance of a task of the utmost difficulty and delicacy, calling for the exercise of a riper judgment and surer discretion than most men have developed at the age of thirty-five. It has been told, though perhaps it is not widely known, that during the Civil War he was sent to Europe with millions to his credit, instructed by the government to purchase arms and munitions of war in order to forestall the purchase of them by the agents of the Confederacy who had been sent over on the same errand; and the confidence which his government had reposed in him was fully justified by the success of his mission.

The business ability displayed by Mr. Hartley was only one of the qualities of character by which he commanded respect. His gifts and benefactions reached an annual sum of which no one had knowledge, unless it were himself, and he was certainly one of those men whose left hand did not know the good his right was doing. Of Hartley House and of the work it accomplishes for the relief of the poor the public has information through annual reports, but we think the major part of Mr. Hartley's giving was private and unrecorded. If it be the rule that the management of large affairs tends to hardness of heart, Mr. Hartley was a splendid exception. Many men enjoyed his friendship, his advice, his encouragement, and his assistance, and we venture to say that none of them will aver that they ever had a friend more true, loyal, and unselfish. It was a warm and full heart that beat in his bosom.

Such a man is an element of strength and safety in any community. The influence which naturally belongs to men of large means he wielded always in a way to set an example of prudence and wise conservatism. He was the guide of men less self-reliant, but not into dangerous paths or unwarrantable ventures. Mr. Hartley will be most seriously missed and his loss will be felt among those who met him, trusted him, and dealt with him in the daily round of affairs. He will be sincerely mourned by those who, through their knowledge of the noble and kindly qualities of his character, had come to feel for him real esteem and affection.

### *From the " Commercial Advertiser "*

MR. HARTLEY'S abilities, services, and sterling personal qualities won for him the esteem and admiration of the strong, able men with whom he was daily thrown into contact. In the higher world of finance he enjoyed an exalted reputation. But fame as it has fallen to many less worthy he never had. To the great multitude he was unknown. His name to the general public, if it meant anything, brought but dim remembrance and vague recognition. Mr. Hartley was one of those great men — for endowments such as his, applied as he applied them, warrant the appellation — who do their work quietly, unostentatiously, who are famous only among the famous.

For fame, in the popular sense, Mr. Hartley cared nothing. The path to that sort of distinction was opened to him, and he turned his face from it. He was often besought by leading men in his party (he was a Republican) to take an active part in politics. His native courage and sound judgment, his tact, his skill in dealing with men, his foresight, were recognized by the men of influence who knew him. These men saw in him great possibilities of political leadership, of political preferment. But Mr. Hartley steadfastly said no to them all. He preferred to devote himself to business, to great commercial and financial enterprises, and to charity. He was a genuinely modest, unassuming man.

His characteristics in that respect were shown most notably in his charities. Every year he gave away great sums of money. How much his donations amounted to annually no one knew but himself, and his individual gifts were known only incidentally. Mr. Hartley was literally content in his works of beneficence not to let his right hand know what his left hand did.

His career furnishes a striking example of the power of concentration, of complete mastery of a subject, as the first essential of great success. Mr. Hartley, when just out of school, entered the counting-room of a leading firm of gun-importers. Before long he was an expert on firearms. He knew his subject not only on its commercial but also on its technical side, and when he was only thirty-five years of age he was selected by Mr. Stanton, President Lincoln's Secretary of War, for the important and responsible position of government agent in Europe, with plenary powers. His mission was to buy firearms from the foreign manufacturers for the Union army. There was no question as to his equipment for that task alone. But his mission was more than a merely commercial one. He was in a real sense committed to a diplomatic service. He was to outwit the agents of the Confederate Government, and win sympathy, much needed, for the Union cause. No small task was that for a young man of thirty-five. That Mr. Hartley succeeded brilliantly in his mission shows that his judgment was extraordinarily matured, and his finesse and tact highly developed.

In the financial world Mr. Hartley was known as one whose advice might well be taken by the most astute, as one on whom the strongest might lean in troublous times, as one who, although possessing in the highest degree courage and self-reliance, might always be found on the side of conservatism and prudence. Dealing daily with large propositions of finance, deciding questions involving dollars alone, he lost none of his human, kindly qualities. He was trusted, esteemed, regarded with affection by all those who knew him.

*From the " Christian Work "*

### GENERAL MARCELLUS HARTLEY

MARCELLUS HARTLEY, who passed away in this city on Wednesday of last week, was not only a most successful man of business, engaged in many departments of business activity, but he was a man of beneficent impulses—deliberate purpose, rather—and gave freely to many beneficent institutions, as he was also an active participant in the management of not a few. Mr. Hartley, too, was a pronounced patriot. At a critical time during our Civil War he went abroad and secured arms for our army, which if any one else could have done, no one, it is safe to say, could have done so well. Not only so, but he refused any and all compensation for himself or his firm, and for this act of patriotism President Lincoln made him a brigadier-general. Perhaps no one has indulged in more charitable acts than Mr. Hartley; and it is certain none could have been more unostentatious in their bestowment. Notwithstanding his multiplied business interests — he was president or director of some fifteen great corporations — Mr. Hartley's heart and mind were deeply fastened upon the claims of charity. Especially noticeable is the Hartley Home, initiated by him, and placed under the management of the New York Association for the Improvement of the Condition of the Poor, the institution being named after the father of the deceased philanthropist. Among the other charitable institutions fostered by Mr. Hartley, all of which owe their existence in part to the work of a member of the Hartley family, are the Society for the Relief of Ruptured and Crippled Children, the Presbyterian Hospital, and the Association for the Improvement of the Condition of the Poor. Because of his unostentation few men saw their names less frequently in the public prints than he; but none the less was he known all through New York circles of business and benevolence as one of New York's foremost citizens. No one, too, enjoyed more the rest and the seclusion of family life than he; and those who have come in contact with him at all to know him will mourn the loss of one possessing noble qualities of head and heart which found expression in personal activities. *Siste Viator!* Well has Sir Thomas Browne exclaimed, " Our very life is but a dream, and while we look around eternity is at hand."

# IV

## EXTRACTS FROM
## MR. HARTLEY'S CORRESPONDENCE
## DURING THE CIVIL WAR

*Note.*—During the nine months that Mr. Hartley was in Europe, in 1862 and 1863, in the service of the United States Government, he wrote a vast number of letters. These are wholly on business affairs, to various manufacturers, to his agents, to his bankers, and, as a rule, they possess little interest to the reader. Among them, however, those to Secretary Stanton, of which there are twenty-five or thirty, and to other persons in high place, stand out as possessing a more than passing interest; they deal with more general questions of policy and with business details of greater moment. A few of those are included in the text of Chapter V. They are here supplemented by some further correspondence of the same sort, introduced with the purpose, not of giving any complete account of Mr. Hartley's doings, but of showing the various aspects of his work.

### No. 9.

BERLIN, October 7, 1862.

*Sir:*

My last was under date of the first instant from Cologne. I have nothing from you since your three favors of the twelfth ulto.—No. 6. I have just received a telegram that the additional £150,000 credit has arrived, making £380,000 in all, but they all expire on the first of November. Please lose no time in extending them until such time beyond the tenth of December as in your judgment you may require me. You will pardon me if I suggest here that it is our right course to secure all arms here in Europe, in order that the South may not obtain them. They are purchasing largely, and wherever they can find arms they purchase, paying but little attention to price as long as they can obtain them. They are endeavoring to purchase Enfields. Some of our Birmingham makers have refused to deliver at less than 53/. The London makers have refused to continue after the first of November at the old price, saying they have been offered more. I refused to listen to an advance, but, since my journey among the different arms manufactories on the Continent, I find that the Confederates are making all efforts to secure a large quantity of arms, and I have written to the London manufacturers and requested Mr. Tomes to obtain the refusal until my return of all they can make until the first of December at their price, as by that time I hope to find out positively if they have a bona fide offer for more than I am paying, and, if so and the offer is from the South, I certainly shall be justified in paying it. So in regard to Birmingham, if their agents are in the market, I think it the part of wisdom to make contracts with the Birmingham manufacturers at such prices as I can get them to sign, binding them down. They would not sign contracts at 45/, and the most of them even at 50/, as they all had been caught so often they preferred to take the chance of the market. Therefore I think if the South has agents purchasing arms, if I can make contracts with the manufacturers to bind them, at prices exceeding your limits, I think it my duty to prevent the arms falling into their hands.

At Liège I purchased ready-made and entirely new arms:

C. DANDOY . . 400 French Rifled Muskets, $\frac{69}{100}$, with implements and extra cones — packing boxes no charge . . . . . . . . 37 fr.

120 ditto, ditto, No. 2 . . . . . 43 fr.

B. M. TAMBEUR ⎱ 2200 ditto, ditto, No. 2, freight
    FRÈRES ⎰ paid to Antwerp — packing boxes 8 fr. . . . . . . . 46.75 fr.

| | | |
|---|---|---|
| ASSOCIATION OF LIÈGE | } 2000 | Piedmontese Rifled Muskets, extra cones, implements; freight free to Antwerp, boxes 8 fr. . . . . . . 48 fr. |
| | 1500 | French Rifled Muskets, with implements as above; freight free to Antwerp, boxes 8 fr. 39 fr. |
| | 800 | ditto, with elevated sights . 42.50 fr. |
| LOUIS MULLER | 3500 | French Rifled Muskets, intended for the Italian Government, all ready for shipment . . . . . . . . 46 fr. |

The above were all made and will be shipped in two weeks, as soon as extra cones and implements can be made. I also ordered 8000 of the same kind from the Association, Dandoy and Mr. Muller to be ready by the first of November of either quality, they to inform me when the lots are ready for purchasing.

That makes in all ordered in Liège of 69/100, 18,520—all of which will leave Europe on or before, say, the fifth of November.

You will be informed from Birmingham weekly how many are shipped and the amount of drafts.

In Vienna I purchased 20,000 blue barrel with angular bayonet, leaf sight, 58/100, and 10,000 bright barrel with angular bayonet, leaf sight, 54/100—including for each case of 20 guns 10 ball screws, 20 combined wrenches, and 20 extra cones at 26 florins—say 53 francs. The arms are all entirely new, but will have to be carefully inspected and packed, as there is no dependence to be placed upon any of the manufacturers. It will take at least six weeks to ship them all.

I found on arrival in Vienna that Boker had the refusal, or, in other words, the control of the arms. I obtained possession of them by agreeing to pay him 40 kreuzers, or about $16 per gun, he paying all expenses, delivered at the railroad. He will have to pay for packing-boxes, viewing (a house will have to be obtained), and banker's commission, which is one-half per cent. All is under the supervision of my Springfield inspector. It is the best arrangement I could make, and under the circumstances very fortunate that he was there, for I should have had to employ some one — a commission house would not have done it except for a commission, and I should be afraid to trust them; my bankers could not do it, and under the circumstances it was very fortunate, as I cannot remain there.

I found that Moses and Co., a London house with a Captain or Colonel Hughes, had purchased 50,000 bright barrel Austrian guns, 54/100 caliber, no leaf sight, from the Austrian government about three weeks since at 26.75 florins, and Mr. Martin of the above firm is now in Vienna attending to the shipment of them. They were in treaty for those I purchased, and no doubt would have purchased them in a little time. The Austrian government refuse to sell any more for the present, but Mr. Truberth, the manufacturer from whom I purchased the arms, the controller of all the manufactories, informs me that when the different contractors make deliveries of the "new arm" the government will no doubt sell more, but it will be some two or three months. He has promised to obtain from the government the refusal of the next lot and inform me.

The South purchased 30,000 in the spring, and now 50,000 more. I was informed in London that samples of the Prussian guns were offered there to the South and they thought of purchasing. On inquiry I found that Hughes was temporarily absent from Vienna, and thinking that he might be here, I started Sunday for this place. The government here offer 50,000 rifled Prussian guns, caliber 72/100, nipples too large, — in other respects it is a good gun, — at 10 Prussian thalers (about $7). They have already three offers for them, — one from Hamburg, — but I cannot find out who is offering.

I have carefully inspected the guns and would not hesitate

one minute if they were the proper caliber. You instruct me to purchase 69/100 if I cannot obtain smaller, but if 69/100 cannot be obtained you leave it to my judgment to purchase such arms as are serviceable. These arms are serviceable, but the bore is the objection. If I allow them to pass now the South will have them. They can be used by the militia, and in an emergency by regular troops. The price, 10 thalers, is rather high. They are not worth, at the outside, over $6. Shall I purchase at $7 or not? I have to decide to-morrow. I am a little perplexed. They are scattered in eleven different arsenals throughout Prussia. I shall have to have packing-boxes made, employ inspectors and viewers for each place — 100,000 thalers to be paid down as a guarantee, the balance at each arsenal on delivery of each lot of guns. Personally I cannot attend to all of it. My Springfield inspector has all he can attend to at Vienna. It would be impossible to have the cones altered here. It would have to be done in New York. All these things are against the arms. Yet I still think it my duty to secure them. The arms, I find, cannot be purchased except by a Prussian subject. This I may arrange with my bankers. I think it advisable to go to one or two of the arsenals—say Stettin and Magdeburg, the nearest—and see the condition they are in before I make an offer.

I now feel the want of more inspectors and trustworthy men. I do not know where to obtain them.

I do not know at present of any more arms of any amount to be obtained in Europe.

I have written to my house in Paris to call upon the French authorities and see if they can or will dispose of any, but there is but little probability of doing anything there. There are some Garibaldis in Hamburg, but they are very inferior. They no doubt will now be sent to New York on speculation.

If I purchase these 50,000 Prussians, the amount purchased by me will be, say, 18,000 in Liège, 30,000 in Vienna, 50,000 in Berlin—98,000 in all.

I send this letter to-night and will endeavor to inform you by same steamer, if possible, in regard to the 50,000.

Yours respectfully,

MARCELLUS HARTLEY.

*To* Hon. E. M. STANTON.

In reading this letter over, I refer to the Confederates being in treaty for the 30,000 purchased in Vienna, implying that as Boker had the control of them he was the party. They were in treaty with Truberth before Boker. Mr. B. informed me that they, Mr. Martin of Moses and Co., had offered them a price for some Garibaldis, but he refused to sell any arms that might go directly or indirectly to the Confederates.

BERLIN, October 7, 1862.

Mr. C. W. MAY,

*My dear Sir:*

I am in receipt of your letter of the 2d inst., as well as that of the 1st at Liège. My object in now writing is to request you, if possible, to find some one who can obtain some arms from the French Minister of War. I thought of B——, but he may think that he might make political capital and write direct to Washington. He would not do, as he holds an official position under our government; and the French government, being neutral, would not have anything to do with him.

You had better see the minister yourself, and in your own name ask him if he will sell any of their arms, and if he will not, call upon Mr. Poirier, the old gentleman, and get him to see the emperor and let him purchase in his own name, or rather see what can be done—how many, price, etc., and description.

Do not say a word to any one about it. Do not take any one's advice about employing B——, as it cannot be done through him. Move quickly. Do not send me any letters with our business stamp upon them. I will inform you where next to write me. Much obliged to Mr. Morgan for his kindness.

Yours truly,

M. HARTLEY.

No. 10.

BERLIN, October 8, 1862.

*Sir :*

I wrote you from this place yesterday. I have just returned from Stettin, where I saw 12,000 of the Prussian rifled 72/100 guns. They are all in good order, nine-tenths of them having never been used. I have concluded to purchase them, and have made an offer of 8 Thl., 5 Sil. gr. They ask ten thalers. I have so arranged it if they refuse I can know what will buy them. It will take two weeks to have cases made and have them packed at Stettin. If I succeed in obtaining them,—and I have little doubt but I shall obtain them,—it will take at least three weeks to pack them—say four weeks before they are all shipped. The nipples will have to be fixed in New York. They all have ball screws, but no wrenches; those you will have to have made in New York.

I examined their cartridge at the arsenal, and if I could judge from appearances, I should say that the ball which they use is not larger than our 69/100, and appeared to be lighter. The concave runs nearly to the top, thus making the ball a mere shell. They use an iron cup in the cavity, but the officers said it was of no use, as the powder expanded the ball sufficiently to fill the grooves. I send a ball by this mail, with instructions to send to you. I am led to make these remarks from what you have written in regard to our troops disliking to shoot the old 69/100. If I remember right, the Minié ball in our cartridge for 69/100 caliber is much heavier than the Prussian

72/100. Our ball is merely concaved, or rather cupped out like the head of a ramrod, thus making the ball much heavier than there is any occasion for and using more lead than is necessary. If the ball was concaved or hollowed out in proportion to the Prussian I believe the soldiers would not complain so much; they certainly would not have so much to carry, and the balls would not cost so much. I may be wrong, but it certainly is worth looking into.

In some instances I have intended the arms to be forwarded without implements and extra cones, but they will be sent in, say, seven to ten days afterwards by themselves. I have instructed S. H. & G. to report these things to Captain Crispin.

The nipples of the Austrian guns will all be fixed on this side, and extra cones will be new, similar size to our Springfield.

Some of the arms shipped from Liège had no elevated sights; it would take from three to four weeks to put them on those that were finished and ready for shipment, so I sent without sights. Those in hand will all have sights; there are not over 4,000 without elevated sights.

With the 50,000 Prussian, I shall have purchased, say, 98,000, but I shall still purchase, if I can find them, say, 5,000 or 10,000 good arms.

The 30,000 Austrian at 53.40 francs will amount to  64,200
"   50,000 Prussian, say, 10 thalers . . . . . . . .  70,000
                                                    ———————
                                                    £134,200

If I continue to keep possession of the Enfield market I shall want, say, £200,000 more by the 10th of December, or, rather, at once, as my purchases end on the 10th of December. In my next I shall be able to give you an account of drafts.

Please let me know as early as possible your decision in regard to the control of the Enfield market after the 10th of December.

If we succeed in shutting off the Confederates from a supply of arms, they must succumb. Had we at the start monopolized all the arms,—suppose it cost ten millions, twenty millions or even more,—where would they have obtained them? If this war is to continue one year, or two, or more, how long will the arms they now have last them? and when they are gone, where will they obtain more? You will pardon me for referring to this again, but from the exertions they are now making here they will clean the market out, and if so, after that we should take care that they do not have any superior arms.

Yours respectfully,

MARCELLUS HARTLEY.

*To* Hon. E. M. STANTON.

No. 12

LIÈGE, October 16, 1862.

*Sir :*

My last was dated 14th inst. from Berlin. I arrived here this morning. Ten thousand new French rifled 69/100 guns have been shipped on the *Hammonia*, to sail 22d inst. from Southampton. The steamer *Bremen*, that was to sail on the 15th, was withdrawn, being disabled. Five thousand more will be ready next week. Prices are advancing here; it was fortunate that I secured the market as I passed through some two weeks since. I have purchased to-day from the Association 1000 rifled 69/100, ready by the 15th of November, with extra cones, freight paid to Antwerp, 42.50 francs, boxes 8 francs, Tanner and Co.; 1500 ditto No. 1, with implements, extra cones, packing-boxes, no charge, by the 14th of November, 45.50; Louis Muller, 2000 Enfields, with cones and packing-boxes, to be delivered weekly all by the 1st of December, 65 francs; B. M. Tambeur Frères, 2000 Untembery government guns, rifles with sights, implements, cones, and packing-boxes, at 40 francs; 10,000 Belgian government muskets, smooth bore (but to be rifled), with implements and cones complete, no charge for packing-boxes, at 37 francs; 5000 ditto with sights, implements, cases, and cones, no charge, at 40 francs.

These last 15,000 are government guns, smooth bore, but they will be rifled; 5000 is all I can have sights put on. The whole to be shipped in six weeks — making in all 17,500 69/100 and 2000 Enfields. They are all first-rate guns, and I have concluded not to purchase the 20,000 Prussians referred to in my last, as those purchased here are superior and will be ready for use at once; besides, the 100,000 will nearly be made up; the balance I shall find somewhere. The amount now stands:

In VIENNA . . 30,000
" BERLIN . . 30,000      96,000, independent of all
" LIÈGE . . 18,500              Enfields.
" LIÈGE, to-day, 17,500

The party referred to in my letter as having 30,000 69/100 for sale turns out to be, as I anticipated, a speculator, and the probability is, I have purchased to-day here some of the guns he offers at 55 francs at 37 francs and 40 francs or 45 francs, etc. I wrote you that I had written to my house in Paris in regard to obtaining some arms from the French government. I inclose a letter from our Mr. May in Paris in regard to it. As my purchases are nearly full now, I cannot press the matter any further, but if you desire more arms they may be obtained. I told him to use Mr. Poirier, of the firm of Poirier Frères, who has a house in New York, and who has a contract with the French government to supply all the food and stores for the Mexican expedition, which he does from New York, and knowing the officials and the French emperor, and being a staunch friend, he might obtain from them what a stranger could not. I have selected the best guns for the order of 100,000 which I could find. There are other guns offered to me, but being in the hands of speculators, I do not follow them up, as it tends only to advance the price for the same guns, and at the same time I have the refusal of the maker. I go from here to Paris to look at some Enfields,— one lot of 2000 at 66 francs, and one lot of 700 at 65 francs,— and return to England on Monday. I now have some inconvenience in not having my credit extended.

Inclosed you have memorandum of arms that may be made in six months on this side and also what may be offered for sale.

Yours respectfully,

MARCELLUS HARTLEY.

*To* Hon. E. M. STANTON.

Statement of the number of arms that probably might be made at the different factories on the Continent and in England in six months:

VIENNA . . . . . . . . . . $10.40
     80,000 In 6 months at, say, 26 florins at
           40 cents . . . . . . . . . $832,000
           The government will sell no more
           until the makers replace what have
           been sold. These arms may be all
           $\frac{68}{100}$ after the first two months.

STAHL, in Germany . . . . . . $10.50
     15,000 Enfields in 6 months, at, say, 15
           thalers at 70 cents . . . . . . 157,500
           They are now engaged on govern-
           ment contracts. They make arms
           equal to the English.

HERZBERG . . . . . . . . . . $11.90
     6,000 Enfields in 6 months, at, say, 17
           thalers, 70 cents . . . . . . 71,400
   ————  These are good arms.        ————
   101,000                                    $1,060,900

*Brought forward,*

| | | |
|---|---|---|
| 101,000 | | $1,060,900 |

LIÈGE:

| | | |
|---|---|---|
| 30,000 | Arms, Enfields and French model assorted, at, say, 55 francs at $11 . The Association have contracts with the English government and other governments until next summer. | 330,000 |

LONDON:

| | | |
|---|---|---|
| 50,000 | Enfields, at, say, 60/, $14.50 . . | 725,000 |

BIRMINGHAM:

| | | |
|---|---|---|
| 140,000 | Enfields, at, say, 55/, $13.50 . . | 1,890,000 |

FRANCE, ST. ETIENNE:

| | | |
|---|---|---|
| 20,000 | Enfields and French model, at, say, 60 francs, $12 . . . . . . . | 240,000 |

| | | |
|---|---|---|
| 341,000 | . . . . . . . . . . . . . | $4,245,900 |
| | 17,050 packing boxes, $2 . | 34,100 |
| | | $4,280,000 |

The different governments of Europe have contracts out for arms. The calculation above is independent of such contracts, being what can be made besides all government contracts. This calculation is the outside amount.

Statement of second-hand arms that may be offered for sale in a few months:

PRUSSIA:

BERLIN . . . . . . . . . $7.00
  22,000 Rifled $\frac{72}{100}$ at, say, 10 thalers . . $154,000
  Same as the 30,000 purchased.

*Brought forward,*

| | | |
|---|---|---|
| 22,000 | | $154,000 |
| DARMSTADT . . . . . . . . $6.30 | | |
| 12,000 Rifled $\frac{88}{100}$ French model, say, 9 thalers . . . . . . . . . | | 75,600 |
| These may be offered for sale when they receive the new arms now contracted for. | | |
| WITTENBURG . . . . . . . $6.30 | | |
| 9,000 Rifled $\frac{88}{100}$ French model, say, 9 thalers . . . . . . . . . | | 56,700 |
| When they receive new arms they may be sold. | | |
| BAVARIA . . . . . . . . . $6.30 | | |
| 7,000 Rifled $\frac{88}{100}$ French model, say, 9 thalers . . . . . . . . . | | 44,100 |
| When they receive new arms. | | |
| 50,000 . . . . . . . . . . . . | | $330,400 |
| 2,500 packing-boxes, say, $2 . . | | 5,000 |
| | | $335,400 |

If the party who has the refusal of the 20,000 Prussians does not take them, they will make the number 70,000.

The English government has a large number of arms that it wants to dispose of, but refuses to sell any at present to any one. How many, I do not know, but 200,000 at least; they are the old English musket, smooth bore and rifled. She probably will not sell while the war lasts.

The French government has a large number of old arms. The emperor has always refused to sell them.

The Russian government sold over 400,000 arms; they were purchased by a Russian at St. Petersburg. They are very inferior, comprising carbines, etc., all smooth bores and only fit for the ironmonger.

LIVERPOOL, October 20, 1862.

Messrs. BROWN, SHIPLEY & CO.,
        Liverpool.

*Gentlemen:*

Will you please quietly inquire of Mr. Inman, or from any other parties who may be able to furnish a steamer, the price per ton they would ask for freight from Hamburg and Southampton to New York if I agreed to furnish a full cargo, and also the number of cases a vessel would carry (size of cases same as are sent you). Please do it in your own name. The Hamburg steamers have just advanced the price to $25, and I am willing to take the risk of filling a ship if the price is not too much.

I should want her to leave Hamburg, say, the 5th of November, and Southampton the 8th inst.

Please give me full particulars, naming the quantity of cases, freight to be paid on this side.

Yours respectfully,

MARCELLUS HARTLEY.

Per Steamer *Persia.*        No. 15.

47 HAMPTON ST.,
BIRMINGHAM, November 8, 1862.

*Sir:*

My last letter was from this place under date of 25th of October, numbered 14. I am still without any advice of additional credit. I hope, however, to receive one by the *Asia;* her letters due here Monday. If not, I shall be obliged to stop purchasing in the open market and confine myself to the engagements made by me for Enfields at 69/100 caliber. I am short to-day, say, £30,000; if I continue purchasing Enfields I shall be just so much more short to meet my contracts. Depending upon the receipt of another credit I have continued keeping possession of the market until I have made engagements to the above amount, beyond the £380,000 opened in my favor.

I regret to inform you that Mr. Inman, the owner of the screw steamers from Liverpool, the line that we have been depending upon to carry our arms, informs us that "until further notice" he will not carry any articles "contraband of war." We had 178 cases there waiting shipment, which we have sent to Southampton to go by the steamer of the 19th. The steamer from Southampton on the 19th is the first one to sail, the Bremen Line having none. This, you will observe, throws all freight on that steamer. We shall ship some 50,000 to 60,000 arms on her. All the arms from other parties will have to go by her. If she falls a prey to the *Alabama* she will be a rich prize. As she does not leave until the 19th from here you might send a vessel to casually look after her. Since my last, we have shipped per steamer *Etna* 3220 Enfields from here, 3280 69/100 caliber from Liège, and per steamer *Teutonia* 4600 Austrian, 54/100 caliber; 3140 Austrian, 58/100 caliber; and 2220 Enfields; amount of Enfields to date 58,200, other arms 21,958. Inclosed you have recapitulation to date. Amount of drafts drawn, £181,957. 13*s.*, 4*d.* This is independent of amounts paid for Prussian and Austrian arms and for credit opened in favor of Tambeur Frères and Tanner and Co.

Will give you account as the goods are shipped. I have opened an additional credit for £15,000 for the Vienna purchase, leaving about £20,000 yet to pay.

I am obliged to close this, being interrupted unexpectedly about our freight.

Yours respectfully,

MARCELLUS HARTLEY.

*To* Hon. E. M. STANTON.

47 HAMPTON ST.,

BIRMINGHAM, November 29, 1862.

*Dear Sir :*

My last was from here under date of the 22d inst., numbered 17. To-day I received a telegram from S. H. & G. saying an additional credit was on the way.

I immediately secured all the ready-made arms in the market at prices varying from 42/ to 50/, say about 6000, at an average price of 45/.

I was obliged to slacken up in purchasing, as my credit would not have held out if all the manufacturers had delivered to time. Under the circumstances, it was just as well. The refusal of Mr. Inman to allow his steamers to carry contraband of war threw all the freight upon the Southampton steamers, and as I had as much as I could ship, it was just as well, as it would not be safe to accumulate arms, without means of shipping them.

I had already secured freight for 950 cases from Southampton, at £4 per ton, freight advanced to £7, 10 per cent. primage. Your telegram in regard to the 69/100 I received in time to stop some 400 cases, which made room for those from here and what were shut out at Liverpool.

The effect of Mr. Inman's refusal upon shippers here was caution, and they slackened up; the consequence was guns here went down. Henderson and some of the manufacturers belonging to the Small Arms Company purchased at 42/ to 48/, and they will go to New York.

I cannot tell the nature of the instructions now due by the *Scotia*, but if you have enough arms for immediate use, would it not be as well either to stop purchasing in New York before the arrival of the steamer *Bavaria*, to sail on the 3d of December, or to reduce the price to, say, $14.50 to $15? I cannot see why we should not as well avail ourselves of the market as to pay the speculators and manufacturers the difference. The Small Arms Company here is up to all dodges. I should like to manage them. Before my arrival here in July a contract could have been made with them at 42/ to 45/; they asked me 65/ on the start, etc.

If you do not stop now prices will advance rapidly again. 42/, exchange at 1.23, would make the cost of guns in New York, say, $12.13; 45/ at same rate, $13. You pay exchange all above 1.23.

If you put the price down or stop, inform me, and I will stop purchase until I can buy at 42/ to 45/ and purchase all they have in hand, and if it is your desire to continue, I would bind them down, agreeing to take what stock they had at the above price, provided they would agree to give me all they could make at one or two months, at same price. The better plan would be to reduce the price, saying that guns can be bought and are now worth 42/, and tell Mr. Naylor that the Small Arms Company are buying at that. This information must not come from me.

I have referred to the above, as I think, if they are sharp, we should be.

I have not paid higher than £5 per ton freight, always threatening to ship by the Bremen or Hamburg Line, as the case would be, but after next week there is no steamer of an opposition line until the 26th of December, so I shall be obliged to pay it, although I have succeeded in obtaining the difference of railroad charges between here and Southampton and Liverpool.

I have not yet disposed of any of the 69/100 caliber; two parties have talked of buying. After Monday I shall be able to give it my personal attention.

Of the 10,000 Enfields ordered in Liège, 4000 only have been delivered. These arms are better than any English-made arms, excepting those of the London Armory Company.

This steamer starting from Bremen, we have no Austrian on board, but have some on the steamer from Hamburg to-day—some 5000.

Inclosed you have duplicate invoices and statement of shipment. Amount of Enfields to date, 70,120; total number of arms, 131,810.

Yours truly,

MARCELLUS HARTLEY.

*To* Hon. E. M. STANTON.

### No. 22

47 HAMPTON ST.,

BIRMINGHAM, December 20, 1862.

*Dear Sir :*

My last was from here under date of the 17th inst., No. 21, containing an offer from the London Armory Company.

I now have the pleasure of inclosing invoices of our last shipment, being the largest and best yet made. By the steamer *Hammonia*, which was to have sailed the 17th inst., from Southampton, but was delayed owing to some disarrangement of her machinery (inclosed you have newspaper account) and sailed to-day, have been shipped

    1,700 interchangeable Enfield rifles
    28,060 hand-made ditto
    10,978 Austrian 54/100 and 58/100 calibers.

The balance of Enfields to make the amount of inclosed invoices will be shipped by steamer *New York*, to sail the 24th inst. from Southampton with the 69/100 calibers, viz:

500 interchangeable Enfields

7,300 hand-made ditto

13,860 French rifled muskets — 69/100.

The above, no doubt, is the largest shipment ever made by one party, or ever obtained in the same time of first-class Enfields, 37,560. I have made every effort here, in London and Liège to obtain all the Enfields in hand. In London and Liège I cleaned the market out, but here could have obtained 5000 more if they could have been viewed. We have worked day and night for the last sixteen days. It has required care and caution to push the manufacturers to this unusual quantity, without materially advancing the price. In London and Liège, though I advanced the price for a short time, I gave them larger orders than they could complete, and bought them at the low price, and in Liège from 2 francs to 5 francs less. Here in Birmingham I started at 42/ on the 29th of November, but had to advance to 50/, or should have lost many of the guns.

I shall not be able to obtain the freight bills of the *Hammonia* and the *New York* until the beginning of the week, which will delay my accounts, but they shall be forwarded with the vouchers next week.

I have not insured any of the arms; they all have arrived in safety, as far as heard from. The shipment by the *Hammonia* is very large and valuable, amounting to, say, £110,000. As this advice will reach you before her arrival, if you think it proper they can be insured in New York.

I have used about £110,000 of the last credit. Amount of

Enfields shipped to date, 110,140; total amount of arms shipped, 204,848.

Yours respectfully,

MARCELLUS HARTLEY.

*To* Hon. E. M. STANTON,
*Secretary of War.*

NEW YORK, February 20, 1864.

Hon. E. M. STANTON,
*Secretary of War,*
Washington.

*Dear Sir :*

Will you please inform me if my accounts for the purchase of arms in Europe have been examined and adjusted? If so, I shall be obliged to you if you will acknowledge the same.

The accounts have been in your possession since, say, the 1st of March last.

Yours respectfully,

MARCELLUS HARTLEY.

CPSIA information can be obtained at www.ICGtesting.com
Printed in the USA
LVOW031128030512

280175LV00007B/31/P